QUARRIE ON RACING

QUARRIE ON RACING

Stuart Quarrie

WATERLINE

Published by Waterline Books
an imprint of Airlife Publishing Ltd
101 Longden Road, Shrewsbury SY3 9EB, England

ISBN 1 85310 300 4

A Sheerstrake production.

A CIP catalogue record for this
book is available from the British Library.

Front cover photograph by Rick Tomlinson

Introduction

I have been a professional sailing coach for over fifteen years and during that time have helped sailors at all levels of ability, working with crews at international level as well as those who are struggling in their local club fleets. I still really enjoy teaching and coaching as well as actual regatta sailing and hope that I have been able to express my pleasure in my writing.

This short book contains some of the tips, techniques and solutions that I have found particularly helpful on the race course and over the years. It is not aimed at any individual level but should provide something for most sailors who are racing.

Some aspects will suit you and your boat, others will not be applicable or will already be known by you and the rest of the crew. The sectional layout with headings for all major paragraphs makes it easy to access the specific subjects in which you are interested. Pick out the areas where you need help, then put the ideas into practice afloat — it is normally best to try out new ideas without the stress of an important race whenever possible.

Whatever level you are sailing at, I hope that this book will help a little towards improving your performance and give some enjoyment at the same time. Good sailing, remember when we have learned all there is to know about the sport, that is the time to give up!

CONTENTS

TACTICS

STARTING
Early at the port end   12
Making space to leeward   12
Shifting gear   14
Do not allow barging   14

BEATING
Ducking a starboard tacker   15
Approaching on the port lay-line   17
Starboard lay-line: how early?   19
Heavy or loose cover?   21
Lee bow tack   22
Avoiding the lee-bow tack   23

REACHING
Clear air is vital   24
Overtaking — early decision   25
Being overtaken   26
Towing   27
Taking a tow   29
Shaking off a tow   32

RUNNING
Look behind   33
Cover downwind   33
Gybe-set?   34

MARK ROUNDING
Inside at the gybe mark   34
Breaking an overlap   36

Luff to close the gap   37
Basic rounding method   38
When slow is best   39

NAVIGATION

PREPARATION

Side deck chart table   40
Extract information before the race   41
Read the sailing instructions   41
Take the charts home   43
Order early   43
Protect your charts   44

STRATEGY

The effect of windshifts: upwind   45
The importance of average wind direction   47
The persistent shift or wind bend   48

BASIC TECHNIQUES

Determining line bias   48
Use of transits   50
Back bearings   50
Clearing lines   51
Shaping a course — all in one go   52
Finding the buoy   53
Tidal wind   53
Speed polar curves   55
Finishing line bias   56

INSTRUMENT SYSTEMS

The essentials   57
The dangers of V.M.G.   58
Calibration   59

The Effect of wind shear   60
Keep your own waypoint information   61
Do not rely totally on electronic navaids   62

CREW-WORK

PREPARATION

Spinnaker packing, method 1 — simple   64
Spinnaker packing, method 2 — in stops   65
Identifying the halyards   66
Keeping halyards untwisted   67
Label the halyard clutches   69
Lead the tripping-line forward   70
Cleats for uphaul and spinnaker halyards
     at the mast   70
Clip sheets and guys together   72
How to clip genoa sheets together   72
Marking the genoa luff   72

FOREDECK

Spinnaker set-up in rough water   73
Guy-run spinnaker drop   75
What type of snap shackle?   76
Double sheets and guys   77
Gybe-set: topping lift position   78
Set up the spinnaker in good time   78
Getting a spare halyard over the pole   79

COCKPIT

Tailing to windward   80
Riding turns on a winch   80
Gybe-set: sheeting the genoa   82
Gybe-set: guy on too soon   82

Make up the new winch 83

GENERAL
Sleeping on the side deck 83
Crew weight in light airs 85
Co-ordination close reaching in a blow 86
Going up the mast 88

HELMING
Feathering to keep her on her feet in a gust 88
Avoiding the rolling crazies 89
Helming upwind in waves 90
Too narrow a groove 92
Are you sitting comfortably . . .? 93

SAIL-TRIM

RIG TUNING
Mast upright? 94
Mast-rake 95
Shroud tension 97
Prebend 98

GENOA
Moving the fairlead under load 100
Reaching sheet 101
Inboard or outboard sheeting upwind? 102
Tell-tales 103
Fore-and-aft sheet lead position 105
Sheet tension 106

MAINSAIL
Upwind sheet tension 107
Crack-off for speed 109

Traveller versus boom vang upwind   109
Use of backstay in gusts   110

SPINNAKER
Airflow over the spinnaker   111
Fore-and-aft pole position   112
Pole height   114
Tweakers   114
Trim for a windy run   115
Concentration   116

GENERAL
Draft position   117
Draft position — special cases   119
Twist in waves   120
Wind shear   122
Leech lines   123

INDEX   125

Tactics

Starting
EARLY AT THE PORT END?

When the start line is biased you may need to start very close to the port end, in which case there is always the possibility of mis-timing your run-in slightly and being early. In many cases, although it is at the port end of the line that you wish to start, it will also pay to get over to the starboard side of the first beat and in these cases, it will not lose you much if you accept the fact that you are early, accelerate out of the position by the port end mark and do a complete circle — gybing around and coming back into the line a little late, but with the ability to stay on port tack having ducked a few starboard tack sterns.

Starting
MAKING SPACE

When you are on the start line in a satisfactory position relative to other boats, you will need to defend your slot, sometimes quite vigorously. At the start itself, the ideal is to have a gap to leeward so that you are able to sail fast away from the line and not have to pinch in order to keep your air clear. Boats close to windward are not so much of a problem unless they are faster than you.

Since you are allowed to luff, (as far as head-to-wind until the gun goes) you can quite easily make a gap to leeward by luffing the boat to windward or just slowing down and letting the boat to leeward sail away. The problem then is how to stop another boat from coming from behind to take the nice gap that you have just created.

So long as you are looking around and become aware that a yacht is coming from behind to fill your gap, you can often dissuade them from so doing by temporarily bearing away to visually fill the gap. As soon as they have passed you can luff into position once more.

The only danger is that you may inadvertently pick up speed while bearing away, so be prepared to ease sheets prior to the manoeuvre.

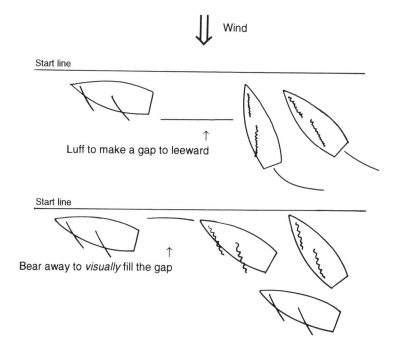

Wind

Start line

Luff to make a gap to leeward

Start line

Bear away to *visually* fill the gap

Starting
SHIFTING GEAR

In most starting situations you will wish to start either with speed — to get into clear air, or to point high to stay in clear air. It is rare to be able to start at your optimum or target speed until you're clear of the crowding near the line.

It is therefore vital that the whole crew understand which mode is required. Either trim for height when there is a yacht close to leeward; or crack sheets slightly and go for speed if there is another yacht about to sail over you to windward.

Once you have got clear, the whole boat should then be re-trimmed to optimise your v.m.g. for the conditions.

Starting
DON'T ALLOW BARGING

The racing rules are very explicit in that a yacht approaching a starting mark has different rights to those given at other buoys. Assuming that the mark is not a continuous obstruction, (eg. if the committee is on the shore) then there is no need for a leeward boat to give water to a windward boat for the start.

This means that a yacht reaching towards the committee boat end of the line has no right to call for water. Until the gun goes, you can hover, head-to-wind if necessary, next to the buoy and deny access to everyone else.

Once the gun has gone the situation suddenly changes.

In my experience this is not appreciated by many club sailors. From the start time until you have cleared the line, you are not allowed to cut someone out at the mark by sailing above your proper course. If you have been sitting quietly with your sails flapping you must, as soon as the starting signal is made, bear away to your proper course (either the compass-course to the first mark or to close-hauled) even if this lets other boats reach in to windward of you.

Beating
DUCKING A STARBOARD TACKER

If you are on port tack going up the beat and are being approached by a starboard tacker on a collision course, you have to decide which of the various options to take in order to "give way". If you feel that it is best to continue on port tack and there is any danger of not being able to cross in front of the starboard tacker then it is best to duck under his stern.

There are basically two ways that this can be done — efficiently so that you lose no ground or in a panic at the last moment when you will lose several boat lengths.

Let's look very briefly at the panic mode first. Although you realise that a duck is necessary any action is delayed as long as possible in the vain hope that he will go away. When within one or two boat lengths from the starboard tacker, you yank the tiller up to windward, keeping the sails pinned in hard, the boat pirouettes around her keel while braking hard both with the rudder and the stalled sails. The starboard tacker goes past really close in the opposite direction so that it is impossible to harden up onto the wind again until he is completely past you. By the time your yacht is back on course and up to speed he is several boat lengths ahead.

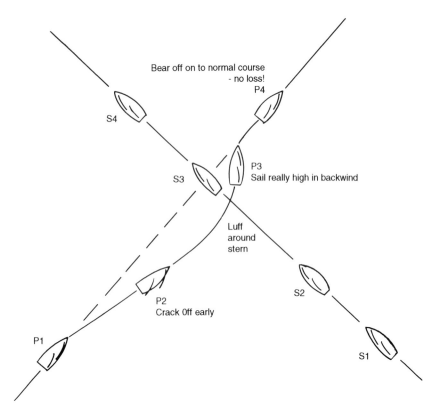

Bear off on to normal course - no loss!
P4

S4

P3
Sail really high in backwind

S3

Luff around stern

S2

P2
Crack Off early

P1

S1

Ducking a starboard tacker

The correct way to duck is to plan ahead and once again to ensure that your trimmers understand what is going on. As soon as you accept that you are going to duck behind the starboard tacker, you should bear away and aim just behind him, easing the sails to keep them trimmed to perfection. Your boat accelerates and your helmsman keeps aiming a little way astern, gradually coming back towards close hauled as the starboard tacker gets closer. As he goes past, you are travelling significantly faster than he is and are in a position to continue your luff around his stern. This means that you can use his back wind to advantage, luffing very hard for a few seconds after he has passed and then bearing away again to your normal close hauled course as your excess speed drops off. If done properly, your sails will have been working all the time and you will have lost nothing at all.

Beating
APPROACHING ON THE PORT LAY-LINE
When rounding the windward mark to port, it is usually best to try to approach with at least a little time on the starboard lay-line in order to facilitate a quick spinnaker hoist. On some occasions though, the situation will force you to approach on port tack right up to the buoy.

Assuming that there is another yacht on the starboard lay-line and that you are going to arrive at the same time, you will have to decide whether to bear off and go behind the starboard tacker or to risk tacking to leeward of him in the hope that you can round the mark inside him.

If you decide on the latter course of action, it is obviously important to understand the rules which will apply. For most practical purposes, the mark can be removed from any calculations so far as your right to tack is concerned. So long as you have completed your tack (ie. borne away to a close hauled course) before the starboard tacker has to start luffing to clear you, then you are in the clear. Your next problem is going to be getting round the mark. Because you are now on the inside of the other yacht and have established a new overlap within two boat lengths of the buoy by completing a tack, you are entitled to claim water. In getting round the buoy you can shoot the mark if necessary but ONLY AS FAR AS HEAD-TO-WIND. If you have misjudged the situation and need to luff beyond head-to-wind, then by definition you are tacking and were not eligible to call for water.

During the second inshore race of the 1987 Admiral's Cup the British yacht *Jamarella* found herself in just such a situation. She had come to the windward mark from the port side of the course and finally tacked inside one of the German team. On this occasion there was a strong cross tide setting the yachts onto the buoy, which made it harder to lay the mark anyway and *Jamarella* had to luff very hard in order to have any chance of rounding the buoy. The German yacht was unable or unwilling to respond adequately and they collided and shortly thereafter *Jamarella* slid sideways onto the buoy. All around who had been watching thought the situation hopeless but in the subsequent protest, a series of photographs of the incident proved that *Jamarella* had not luffed beyond head to wind, thus it was shown that the German yacht did not give enough room for her to round the buoy and it was the German yacht that was penalised.

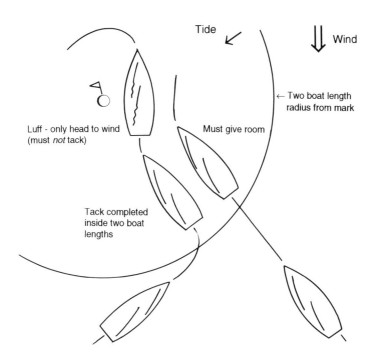

Beating
STARBOARD LAY-LINE — HOW EARLY?

If the top mark is going to be left to port then in most cases you will probably want to arrive on the starboard lay-line in time to facilitate a fast spinnaker hoist. The problem is deciding just how early is sensible.

If you hit the lay-line too late, possibly even approaching close to the port lay-line, you may encounter all the problems described on page 17. If on the other hand you elect to get on the starboard lay-line really early, this also may create its own problems.

To start with, as soon as you are on either lay-line you are locked in to the wind as it is at that time. A lift will just mean that you have overstood the mark and therefore reach in, whereas if you experience a header and are very close to the lay-line, it is going to be dangerous to tack in case the wind shifts back again.

Being on the lay-line for too long also gives the rest of the fleet more opportunities to attack you. Yachts can look at your position and make a fairly good judgement as to whether you are only just laying the buoy or if you have overstood. In the former case, if they are ahead of you they will sail a little past your line before tacking and then give you dirty air all the way to the buoy. In the latter situation, when you have overstood, others can tack under your line and get inside you.

Your defence is to try to confuse the opposition — aiming a bit low if you have overstood and want to persuade another yacht to sail beyond your line or pointing really high for a moment if you are struggling to lay the mark and want a competitor to tack underneath your line.

So, as a general rule, too early on the lay-line, while being easy, will often let the opposition in, whereas being too late makes it difficult if there is bunching and makes the spinnaker set harder.

Beating
HEAVY OR LOOSE COVER?

When you are approaching a competitor while going up the beat and you realise that he is on the making tack, you will have a choice to make. Should you cover him in a heavy manner so as to give him dirt and force him to tack away — or would it be better to put a loose cover on him to encourage him to go the same way as you?

The normal reaction of most port tackers in the middle of the fleet will be to attempt to lee bow tack the starboard tacker and then force him to tack away. The similar reaction of the majority of starboard tackers will be to try to get just ahead of a port tacker, then tack on top of him, give him dirt and thus once again, force him to tack.

Having said that those are the typical mid-fleet reactions implies that they are wrong. In fact they are often the best tactics to force the opposition to go the other way, especially if you are sure about which is the favoured tack. There are two situations however, when it would be better to put on a loose cover by tacking on to the making tack but in such a way so as not to give the other boat dirty wind. The first occasion is if you are not really sure which tack is favoured and you therefore risk sending your opponent into a better situation by forcing him to tack. The second situation when it is best to let the opposition come with you, is when you know you can beat him in a straight on-the-water duel.

There is also a third situation when it can be better to have a close competitor with you, and that is in a long race when it will add measurably to your own performance by having a sparring partner close by.

Beating
LEE BOW TACK

Let's look at the lee bow tack through the eyes of the port tacker. He is approaching a competitor who is on starboard tack and although he is marginally ahead will not be able to cross in front of the starboard boat. He decides that the best plan is to tack close under the other boat's lee bow, attempting to give him as much back-wind as possible and thus force the other boat to tack away.

The manoeuvre will only work if he has good boat speed before the tack and if he is either of similar size or bigger than the starboard tacker. The port tack boat must also be at least level with his competitor and preferably a little ahead. Unless all these criteria are satisfied the manoeuvre is doomed to failure.

If possible, bear away a touch before the tack to increase speed and ensure that your crew know the game plan. The tack needs to be smooth and should be completed within about half a boat length of the starboard tacker. Much closer and you run the risk of being protested out for having infringed rule 41, much further away and your back-wind will be ineffective.

After the tack, it is vital to prevent your opponent

from sailing over you to windward, so you must regain speed as soon as possible. Initially you should sail low with the sails eased a touch until you have at least the same speed as the other boat. Once you have achieved parity of speed it is then possible to gradually tighten everything in and slowly squeeze up to windward. If all has gone according to plan, the other boat will not be able to point high enough to live in your back-wind and he will be forced to tack away.

The dangers of this manoeuvre are twofold. The first has already been dealt with above in that if you tack too late, you may be protested out of the race. The second and perhaps more important danger is that if you fail to squeeze your opponent out, he will probably sail over you to windward and you will be forced to tack again. Not only will this send you the wrong way, but two tacks in close succession is always slow.

Beating
AVOIDING A LEE BOW TACK

Previously, the lee bow tack was considered from the point of view of the port tacker. It is also worth looking at the same situation from the starboard tackers view.

When on starboard tack and approaching a port tacker on a collision course, you must be aware that he may decide to tack under your lee bow and attempt to force you to tack away. If you were about to tack anyway then let him, he will then not affect you after the tack. If on the other hand you want to stay on starboard tack, you should try to prevent him from succeeding in his plan. If he looks as if he will almost cross ahead, wave him on. This call has no legal validity but can often persuade a port tacker not to tack. It is the same logic as flashing your car headlights, which does not mean that another car has to obey you — but it often does.

If it becomes obvious that he intends to tack and is setting up for a close tack, then you can still upset his plans in several ways. Bear away a little and crack sheets to increase your speed and force him to tack earlier than he planned. As he commences his tack, sheet in hard and point as high as possible. This will increase the distance between you so that you can return to your optimum upwind trim. Get the genoa trimmer to monitor the continuing situation so that the helmsman can concentrate properly. If you have done all this then he will probably be unable to squeeze you out and ultimately you will sail past him. However, if you realize that he has been success-ful then tack away as soon as possible, all the time you are in his back-wind you are effectively going backwards.

Reaching
CLEAR AIR IS VITAL

Reaching is generally quite straightforward and there are fewer pitfalls for the unwary than on the beat. One critical factor however, is to keep clear air.

If you allow other yachts to sail directly to windward of you, then you will be sailing in their disturbed wind shadows. These extend a considerable distance to leeward, perhaps as much as 8–10 boat lengths. In many circumstances it may be difficult to feel or see the effect of this, but sailing in dirt means that you will be going slower than normal. When there is a similar sized yacht to windward of you it is often possible to sail below your optimum speed for many miles without realizing it.

To decide if you are in a wind shadow, look at the direction of the windex of the yacht to windward. If its tail is pointing at you then you can be fairly sure you are in disturbed air.

Reaching
OVERTAKING — EARLY DECISION

If you approach a slower yacht to overtake her on a reach and do what half the yachts afloat seem to do — that is to get close up behind before deciding whether to go through to windward or leeward — then you deserve to be either luffed or not to get through.

When approaching the slower yacht, the earlier that you decide which side you are going to attempt to overtake, the better. In general terms it will obviously be faster to get through to windward, but the slower yacht is free to luff you as she pleases until you get to "mast-abeam". This means that if you are going to go through upwind, you must give yourself enough separation between the yachts to render any luffing on her part ineffective. If she is looking behind and sees you starting to climb when you are still a fair distance astern, she may decide to ignore you and let you go past. However, if she decides to fight you and follows your climb to windward, it becomes obvious that a luffing match is about to ensue. Then, it is nearly always better to accept "defeat" gracefully, crack-off and go through far enough to leeward to minimise the effect of her dirt. If the yacht being overtaken is much smaller, then it is possible to go through close to leeward without fear of being stopped by her wind shadow, but she would need to be considerably smaller or slower to allow this to happen.

Reaching
BEING OVERTAKEN

When you are about to be overtaken by a faster yacht, you can force him to go whichever side of you is preferred. This will normally mean coercing him to go through to leeward. In order to be able to do this it is vital to have someone looking constantly astern at the opposition, so that you can see and anticipate any overtaking moves before they get too close.

If you see a yacht either coming directly along your line or slowly climbing out to windward on your hip to overtake to windward, you have the option of signifying to the overtaking boat whether or not you are prepared to accept this. If you make an early alteration to windward, and as he climbs higher you respond, it should quickly become apparent that you will not allow him to go through unchallenged. In most cases this will be sufficient to deter the overtaker and he will drop down to leeward and attempt to go through on that side.

If the overtaking boat has decided to go through to leeward, then he will not affect your speed but if he is in your class, you will wish to slow his progress. While he is more than 3 boat lengths away, you are entitled to sail as you please and can sag down toward his line — even if this means sailing below your "proper course". Once he is closer than 3 boat lengths you are not permitted to sail low and must then resume your proper course even if that allows him through.

Reaching
TOWING

Since all yachts drag a significant volume of water with them in the form of bow and stern waves and because these, like any other waves have a rotating motion of water within the wave, it is possible for a slower yacht to take a tow on the stern wave of a faster one. The bigger and heavier the yacht, the more water she will drag with her and the easier it will be to be towed. Similarly, the lighter you are, the easier it will be to initiate and maintain what is effectively surfing.

In my experience, unless your yacht is ultra light with a powerful rig, it will not be possible to pick up the tow from an overtaking yacht if the difference in boatspeed is more than about a knot. Once on the stern wave however, it is feasible to be towed with a much higher speed differential.

Look behind a yacht travelling at speed and you will see a pattern of waves coming from her stern. There will be the primary stern wave, actually "attached" to the stern itself, and then there will be all the left-over, secondary waves. These secondary waves get smaller and smaller as you get further behind the yacht until eventually they peter out altogether. When trying to get a tow, it is therefore easiest to get onto the primary stern wave since every wave you are behind that, will make it that much harder to maintain the tow.

Two anecdotes are probably worth recounting to show the benefits and disadvantages of towing. In the first, I was skippering a ¾-tonner in an offshore race where the last leg was a 60 mile spinnaker reach in about 15 knots of breeze. We were being overhauled by a Swan 51 which was going about a knot faster than us, so we decided to take a tow. 30 miles later we were still there, less than 2 metres off her transom, having gained several miles on our opposition.

In the second case, I was sailing a Swan 53 when a J-24 decided to take a tow. He stayed with us for some time until eventually he made a mistake and lost the tow, at which time he planed past us anyway and disappeared into the distance ahead. He had miscalculated and although we were initially faster, thus making the tow worthwhile, the wind had picked up and this turned the balance somewhat.

The message is clear — although a tow can give you a huge advantage, make sure that it is helping you because once locked into a stern wave it is often difficult to get out.

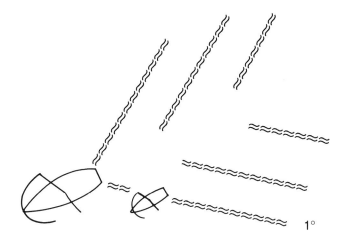

1°

Wave pattern behind a yacht.
1° stern wave is best for a tow
- as close to the towing yacht as possible.

Reaching
TAKING A TOW

If you are about to be overtaken by a larger/faster yacht which is on the same course, you must decide as early as possible if it is feasible and worthwhile to attempt to get a tow. The larger yacht must be travelling at ,or close to her hull speed or she will not be dragging sufficient water with her and you should not need to deviate too much from your course or the exercise will probably not be worthwhile.

Once you decide to try to get on her stern wave, the next consideration is "which side, to windward or to leeward?". Normally as the diagrams show, if the wind is near the beam, you should be on the towing boats windward quarter, while with the wind well aft you should make for her leeward quarter so as not to blanket her sails.

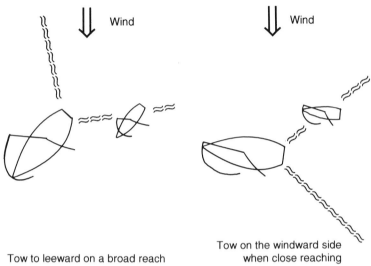

Tow to leeward on a broad reach

Tow on the windward side when close reaching

In attempting to pick up a tow, there are two basic possibilities. If the yacht is significantly bigger than you, it may be necessary to slow her down a little to enable you to get on her stern wave. You should make her pass to leeward of your course and try to sag down onto her stern wave as she passes. Your dirty wind will slow her a little, maybe just enough to start the tow. Once you are locked in, it doesn't matter if she accelerates again because it should be possible to stay with her.

When the overtaking yacht is only a little faster than you, she may never get through if you force her to go to leeward, so you should allow her to go through upwind of you. Your problem here is that you will be blanketed and slowed down as she overtakes and this may make the speed differential too great as her stern wave goes past. In these circumstances it is normally best to soak off to leeward by several boat lengths to reduce the effect of her dirt and then a soon as you feel the effect of her sails reach up hard onto her transom. This gives you maximum speed as her stern wave reaches you and at this moment you should bear away again to initiate the surf. Your sail-trimmers will have to be well briefed and will have to work really hard until you are locked in. Do not forget that as you pick up the wave, your speed should increase and so your apparent wind angle will go forward. This will necessitate trimming-on quite a lot and probably easing the spinnaker pole forward as well.

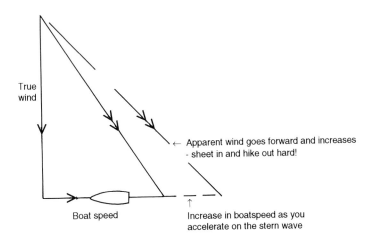

True wind

← Apparent wind goes forward and increases - sheet in and hike out hard!

Boat speed

Increase in boatspeed as you accelerate on the stern wave

Reaching
SHAKING OFF A TOW

If you have a smaller yacht towing in your stern wave it is a moot point whether this will slow you down. My view is that because of the relatively weak bonding between the water and the hull there must be some slowing effect but probably not very much. Therefore if the yacht being towed is much smaller and is not in your class, then it is not worth trying to throw them off. If, however, she is only a little smaller or is in your class, then you should try to get rid of her whenever possible because she will be gaining by the tow even if you are not losing significantly.

On a fairly close reach it should be possible to get rid of the problem with one hard luff followed by a big bear away back to your course. If she is on your weather quarter, it may even be possible to get your rig to touch her spinnaker when you luff, thus putting her into a situation where she can be protested. If you do this and she doesn't exonerate herself or retire, you MUST protest or a third party could protest you both for having had a collision.

When the wind is further aft and you are both on a broad reach it is much harder to throw off a towing yacht. However you alter course, she will be able to respond and you will end up by just slowing both of you down. In most cases there is little option but to settle down and ignore the other yacht.

Running
LOOK BEHIND

When on a run it is vital to remember that:–
a) The wind is coming from behind.
b) windshift, gust and lulls approach from behind.
c) The opposition are overtaking from behind.
d) Dirty air comes from behind.

This all means that while it is obviously still important to look ahead it is also absolutely vital to keep a good look-out astern. Watch the opposition and anticipate their moves so that no-one steals a march on you. Watch both the opposition and waves etc. for indications of forthcoming changes in wind to enable you to maximise your advantage.

In short, make sure that someone who understands tactics is continually looking behind while you go down any run.

Running
COVER DOWNWIND

Keeping your opposition covered is just as important while running as it is was when on the beat. The difficulty is that while it is easy to cover yachts behind you when going upwind, the tactical advantage tends to be reversed on a run.

It will always be the yacht astern who is able to put "heavy" cover on another yacht by sailing directly upwind of her, giving her dirty air and forcing her to gybe away. All you are able to do from a position in front is to put a loose cover on the opposition by staying between them and the mark or by staying on the preferred side of the course, but you are not in a position to herd the yachts behind.

Running
GYBE-SET?

Have you ever watched a match race? If you have, then you will have seen that the first yacht to the windward mark will nearly always set their spinnaker with a gybe-set rather than a bear-away set. The reason for this is the importance match racers place on being inside at the leeward mark, so that they are able to round inside. As the race gets longer, this becomes less and less important but on ordinary inshore races it is still worth considering especially if the fleet is large and close together.

The other reason for deciding on a gybe-set is when the wind direction dictates that you should come away from the top mark on the opposite gybe. For example, the run may be very lop-sided with only a short starboard gybe and a much longer time on port gybe.

Mark Rounding
INSIDE AT
THE GYBE MARK

As you approach the gybe mark it is important that you do not end up going round and outside a pack of other yachts. If you are forced into this situation, you will not only travel much further than the inside boats but you will also end up to leeward, in dirty wind after the mark.

One example will show just how important it is not to be outside. During the second inshore race of the 1987 Admiral's Cup, the British yacht *Juno* was coming into the gybe mark with a whole lot of other One Tonners and had manoeuvred herself into an inside position. By the crucial 2 boat length circle from the mark, the yacht just outside her claimed to have broken the overlap and squeezed *Juno* out so that she had to go round outside the whole bunch of other yachts. She ended up losing nine places on this one mark rounding. Incidentally she was unable to prove that the other yacht shut her out in the subsequent protest.

If you have been trying to overtake another yacht to windward but are unable to get clear ahead by the time the gybe mark is approaching, it is usually the best policy to duck out early, deliberately slow down enough to enable the inside yacht to break the overlap and then work onto the inside of her. If you time things well you may be able to establish an inside overlap before reaching the critical two boat lengths of the mark. In this case you can claim water. Even if you don't get an inside overlap, the worst case will now be that you follow the other yacht round the mark and if your gybe is better than hers you should be in a position to attack her immediately after the rounding.

If you have left things too late and are coming into the mark itself on the outside of another yacht, all is not lost — yet. Luff up to separate yourself from the inside yacht and then do a really smooth, wide gybe. She will be pressurised into doing a tighter reach to reach gybe inside you and may well find this difficult, whereas your gybe can be an easy, reach-run-reach without undue pressure. In many cases by doing a better gybe, you will still end up to windward and right on her hip after the rounding.

Mark Rounding
BREAKING
AN OVERLAP

Rule 42 deals in detail with the rights that an outside yacht must give an inside opponent at marks (and obstructions). One of the basic tenets though, is that if an outside yacht is overlapped by an inside one as they reach a position two boat lengths from the mark, then the outside yacht must give the inside yacht room to round the buoy.

In many situations an overlap will be fairly tenuous, with first one yacht and then the other surging forward and maybe with only a small amount of overlap anyway. In this sort of situation, it may be possible for the yacht on the outside to deliberately break the overlap just before the yachts enter the two boat length circle, thus enabling her to deny the other yacht room.

An overlap is determined by taking a line perpendicular to the fore-and-aft line of the yacht, from the furthest aft point on the yacht ahead as shown in the diagram. If any part of the yacht astern overlaps this line then the yachts are said to be overlapped.

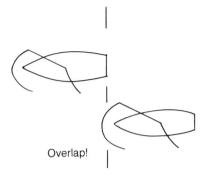

Overlap!

It is therefore possible to break an overlap merely by altering your course so as to bring this imaginary line further ahead, normally by momentarily turning away from the mark.

Unfortunately for the outside yacht in this situation, the onus of proof will be on her to establish that the overlap was in fact broken and that it was broken while the yachts were further than two boat lengths from the buoy.

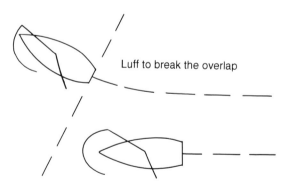

Luff to break the overlap

Mark Rounding
LUFF TO CLOSE THE GAP

If you have rounded the leeward mark just ahead of another yacht, then in most circumstances you should have attempted to come away from the mark as tight as possible so as not to leave a gap for the other yacht to sail into. This in itself should ensure that he cannot actually overtake you while you are rounding the buoy.

However, unless you are careful it is still possible for the yacht behind to snatch the advantage. If the yacht astern manages to get a little bit to weather of your course as you both settle into the beat, she will prevent you from tacking, since to do so would be against rule 41.

The way to prevent this is not only to perform a neat mark rounding but also to ensure that you come out of the rounding with plenty of speed to enable you to luff sharply just after the buoy, thus putting you half a boat length to windward of where you would have otherwise been. This manoeuvre will make it very hard for the other yacht to get to windward of you.

Mark Rounding
BASIC ROUNDING METHOD

In nearly all mark rounding situations you will want to leave the mark as tightly as possible, either to close the gap on your opposition, to be as far upwind as possible or whatever. This means that it is normally best to plan your approach so that any manoeuvre (such as gybing) is done before the actual rounding thus enabling you to come away from the mark nicely. In most cases, your approach will be relatively wide and your departure tight — as in the diagram.

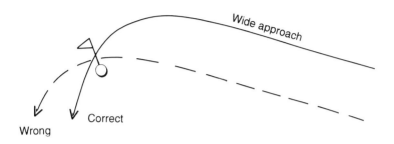

Mark Rounding
WHEN SLOW IS BEST

If approaching a mark with a yacht just ahead as you get within two boat lengths of the buoy, then you must either stay behind her or round the buoy on the outside. In nearly every case it will be a better compromise to stay behind and at worst follow the other yacht round, rather than being forced to sail a longer distance and probably end up in dirty air, possibly having let other yachts through on the inside as well.

This is one of the classic cases where it can really pay to slow down, spilling wind, dropping your spinnaker early or whatever else is appropriate to avoid getting into an overlapped situation.

Obviously if you are able to get an inside overlap more than two boat lengths from the buoy, then this is better still!

Navigation

Preparation
SIDE DECK CHART TABLE

If you wish to navigate on a modern racing yacht, you must be able to perform for most of the time while sitting hard out on the side deck. I have found that a small, portable chart table is an important element of my equipment.

In its simplest form, a suitable chart table or plotting board could just be a piece of plywood or similar material, with a couple of hooks on the top corners for attachment to the lifelines. On most boats, a board of 18″ x 12″ (450mm x 300mm) is about the right size.

I like to have a pocket attached to the rear of the board for holding charts, pencils and the other bits and pieces of paraphernalia which I might need, and have found one of the proprietary navigator's briefcases to be ideal for the purpose. Glued or screwed onto the board, it holds everything in place without being too bulky.

My chart table is completed with a clip at the top and some elastic straps across the front of the board to hold the current chart in position.

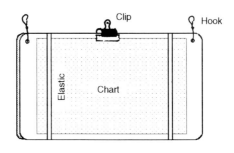

Preparation
EXTRACT INFORMATION BEFORE THE RACE

Anyone who has done any cruising navigation will realise that the information required to navigate around a racecourse, specially for offshore races, is contained in a relatively large number of disparate publications. On a racing yacht, and particularly on the side deck of such a yacht, it is unnecessarily difficult and time consuming to use almanacs, pilot books and the like. Also the weight of the various tomes required is out of all proportion to their usefulness, but some information is undoubtedly essential.

I like to extract the information required from all the various books, copy it on to single sheets and then put together a loose-leaf information book with just the information required for the race. The choice of what information is actually needed will be a case of personal preference and will depend on the race or event being sailed.

The individual sheets can either be put into clear plastic folders or alternatively waterproof photocopy paper can be used.

Preparation
READ THE SAILING INSTRUCTIONS

To say "read the sailing instructions" sounds very much like telling grandmother to suck eggs. However I think that it is so important that it is worth saying here (and repeating to yourself occasionally during the season).

The importance of properly reading and inwardly digesting the sailing instructions was brought home to me very forcibly in a race a few years back. I was going to navigate a certain red and white Class One yacht just for a one-off, offshore race, but with a crew who I had sailed with on other previous occasions. The owner suggested that they picked me up from another yacht near the start line. Since that was most convenient and because I was not the regular navigator, the sailing instructions were not sent to me and therefore I had not seen them until I got on board about an hour before the start. This race was one of the Royal Ocean Racing Club races and the courses for all races during the year were contained in the year-book which I had at home. I had thus prepared for the race on the basis of the year-book. I got on board and quickly scanned the sailing instructions but didn't even look at the course — I "knew" that already!

We sailed the first 180 miles of this 200 mile race and ended up nicely ahead of the rest of the fleet. Coming round the south of the Isle of Wight at night, we headed out to the last turning mark, Nab Tower, feeling pretty good with the world. About 45 minutes later, the next two yachts reached the bottom corner of the island and turned sharp left instead of following us, so I went below to check the course with a sinking heart. Sure enough, in the Sailing Instructions, Nab Tower had been replaced with Bembridge Ledge buoy to cut 10 miles off the course — we ended up 4th instead of first and I learnt an important lesson!

My advice is for the navigator to read the instructions and highlight any important points, then for the skipper to read them, note the points already raised and highlight any which he feels are important. Then both people should go through the instructions together. Apart from anything else, this reduces the responsibility on one person.

Preparation
TAKE CHARTS HOME

If you regularly navigate on one yacht you should take responsibility for the charts and other navigational gear. In this situation, I like to take all the charts home with me after a race so that I can check them before the next race, get replacements where necessary, put on corrections and also plan the next weekend before getting down to the yacht.

The only downside to this, is on the rare occasions when you, as the regular navigator, cannot make a race for some reason; the yacht could be left without any charts on board.

Preparation
ORDER CHARTS EARLY

During the 1979 Fastnet, the yacht I was navigating was sunk by a huge wave. At the time we were about 50 miles off the Irish coast and had made the decision to stay at sea for safety. One of the contributing factors to this decision, was the fact that the hydrographic department of the Admiralty had been on a work to rule for several weeks before the race and large-scale charts of Southern Ireland were not available at the end of July. We only had a small scale metric chart of the area, which for reasons connected with the work to rule was not in colour. This made it very difficult to identify a safe harbour of refuge in the prevailing conditions, so we stayed at sea as the "safe" alternative. Had we had larger scale charts, with the benefit of colour, then we might have made a different decision and headed for Cork harbour — maybe?

The lesson to be learnt from that experience is that charts for major events need to be ordered and collected in plenty of time. Nowadays, as soon as I know that I might be doing a particular event, I discuss my likely chart requirements with the local chart agent who can advise me of any potential problems. Don't leave it too late, especially for major events where there might be a sudden rush on a particular chart number, or you might end up without the required charts.

Preparation
PROTECT YOUR CHARTS

Most charts in use at the present time are made of ordinary paper and when used on deck on a breezy day they do not last very long. One good wave or a short downpour of rain will ruin any chart that is not waterproofed in some way.

There are basically four ways that you can protect a chart from water damage.

a) You can use it either down below at all times. This prevents you navigating from the side deck and is not to be recommended.

b) The charts can all be used within a plastic chart case while on deck. This is easy in theory, but in practice the area of the chart that you need to see will always (by "Sod's Law") be folded under and you will therefore have to remove the chart from the case in order to refold it. At this point the same law states that a wave is bound to come on board and soak the chart anyway!

c) The charts can be laminated with plastic. For small local chartlets and for things like tidal atlases, laminating works exceptionally well. The disadvantage for full size charts is that they tend to become totally unwieldy since a laminated chart will not fold easily.

d) The method of waterproofing which I favour, is to use a spirit based lacquer of the kind used by hill walkers to coat their walking maps. This can be obtained at most chandlers (or cheaper at good camping shops) and normally comes as a spray. It allows the charts to be used as normal and prolongs their life dramatically.

Strategy
EFFECT OF A WINDSHIFT UPWIND
When sailing upwind we are usually trying to get as far upwind as quickly as we can. If the wind is steady then it doesn't matter which tack we are on or which route we take to get to the windward mark. However, if the wind shifts, then we are suddenly presented with huge potential differences depending on whether we are the right or wrong side of the shift.

As can be seen in the diagram, the gains to be made by

getting the shift right are very significant. If there was to be just one windshift all the way up the beat, we should sail towards it so as to be further upwind after the shift.

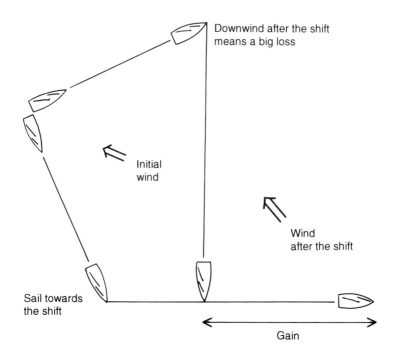

Downwind after the shift means a big loss

Initial wind

Wind after the shift

Sail towards the shift

Gain

Strategy
THE IMPORTANCE OF THE AVERAGE WIND DIRECTION

If the wind shifts more than once up the beat which is normally the situation, then we must be careful not to make short term gains at the expense of an overall loss.

Although it is very tempting to look at each windshift as it comes along and compare the new wind with the wind you have just been sailing in, historical information about wind direction should not be the deciding factor. If we pretend for a moment that there is an accurate crystal ball on board our yacht, then what we should be doing is looking at the wind for the rest of the beat and determining the mean wind direction FOR THE FUTURE. Then if the windshift puts the wind to the right of this "mean" figure we should be on starboard tack, whereas if it puts it to the left then we should be on port tack.

Persistent shift(or wind bend) - look for mean(average) direction

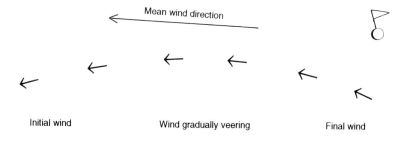

Mean wind direction

Initial wind   Wind gradually veering   Final wind

Strategy
THE PERSISTENT SHIFT OR WIND BEND

When the wind shifts persistently in one direction, either over a period of time or due to a geographical feature, it becomes even more important than usual to consider the average wind, from your position to the windward mark.

Take a day with a sea breeze as an example. The wind might come in initially at about right angles to the coast but as the day wears on, the sea breeze will gradually veer (in the northern hemisphere) until it ends up almost parallel to the coast. This is a persistent shift to the right and it is important to appreciate that the overall pattern is developing, rather than to consider each minor shift individually. Although the general pattern will be for the wind to continue to veer more and more during the day, there will inevitably be small left hand shifts at times.

The old adage of — sail deep into a wind bend — holds true. If it is a bend or persistent shift and you tack on the first shift, you will end up on the wrong side of the eventual wind direction.

Basic Techniques
DETERMINING LINE BIAS

With an upwind start, the most crucial factor to consider is normally, the bias of the line relative to the wind. If the current/tide is even over the width of the line, it can be disregarded (see "tidal wind") and it is the angle that the line makes to the sailing wind which needs to be considered.

Assuming that you have a compass in your boat, the method that I would use to determine the favoured end is as follows:–

When the starting line has been laid, either sail along the line or sight along the line with a hand-bearing compass and note the bearing of the line. Subtract 90° from the bearing which will give the direction that the wind needs to be for a square line. Thereafter, look at the wind direction (by shooting head-to-wind, looking at the compass during a tack or by the use of sophisticated instruments) and a simple comparison with your "square wind direction" will determine which end of the line is favoured. If the actual wind direction is to the left of the "square wind direction" then the port end is favoured and vice-versa.

Example.   Line bearing is 300°.
300°–90° is 210° (square wind)
Actual wind is 205°, therefore the line has 5° of port bias.

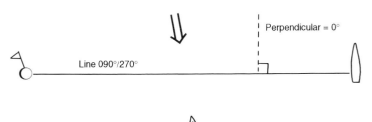

Perpendicular = 0°

Line 090°/270°

Head to wind at 350°
∴ 10° port bias

Basic Techniques
USE OF TRANSITS

Transits; that is lining up two fixed objects to give a position line, provide a very powerful form of visual navigation which can be utilised in many different ways.

At the start, a transit using the limit mark and a shore object gives you an accurate line even when you are unable to see both ends of the line in the melee before the start. This is essential, so that the bowman can call you down to the line in measurements of boat lengths.

"Are we laying the mark?". This is an oft heard question when approaching a mark in a cross-tide. It is possible to take a bearing of the mark with a hand-bearing compass and if this stays constant then you must be laying the mark. This does mean that someone must continually watch the bearing as you approach — also it is often difficult to tell when the bearing is changing by only a few degrees. Here, a transit tells you very quickly and easily if you have allowed enough for the current. If the buoy and the land behind it stay on the same transit then you are OK. If not then the course needs to be altered until they remain steady, relative to each other.

Basic Techniques
BACK BEARINGS

Having rounded a mark in a cross-tide situation, you should have shaped a course to allow for the tide beforehand — but is the allowance correct? Assuming that you know what the rhumb line course was, you can take back bearings from the buoy as you leave it and check that you are staying on that line as an initial check. When sailing inshore, you should revert to using a transit with the next mark as soon as you can see it — but even here a back bearing can be a useful first check.

Basic Techniques
CLEARING LINES

When sailing close to dangers there are often times when you need to know if you are clear of a particular hazard, however you do not actually need to know your position. In these cases a clearing line is often the easiest method of "navigation".

Take the situation as in the diagram. You must stay outside the clearing line in order to be safe from the rocks but it doesn't matter exactly where you are. This sort of clearing line can be derived from many sources but will often be either a bearing on a prominent point or ideally will be a transit between two points, since this allows you to be sure of safety with virtually no effort.

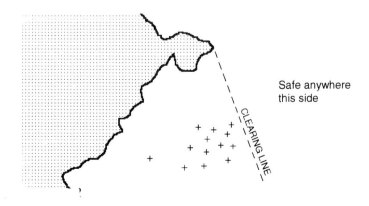

Safe anywhere this side

CLEARING LINE

Basic Techniques
SHAPING A COURSE — ALL IN ONE GO

When sailing across the tide in a situation where the tide will vary before you reach the next mark, it is important to allow for all the differing tidal directions and strengths as a combined vector, so that one course can be steered for the whole leg.

If you allow for each tide or current in turn, so that you stay on the rhumb line, it will invariably increase the distance sailed through the water. This therefore slows your eventual progress. The diagrams are pretty well self-explanatory. If you consider the extreme case, you will see that when both tidal streams are accounted for together you reach the mark in two hours, whereas if each tide is allowed for individually — you never even leave your start point!

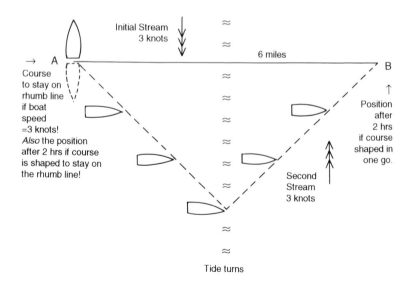

Basic Techniques
FINDING THE BUOY

It sometimes amazes me, when sailing on different yachts and we are looking for a particular buoy that the navigator has no real idea in which direction to look or how far away the buoy should be.

The basic principle of finding an object, such as a buoy, is to know (on the chart) what your relative position, distance and bearing is to that object. If you already have the buoy marked on the chart and you then plot your own position, you should easily be able to ascertain the bearing and distance to the buoy. Remember that if you are close to the buoy, small fixing errors can create large errors in the bearing.

In many races the committee lays a mark and I always plot its position on the chart before starting the race. I also like to plot the start line position, particularly if the same line will be used for the finish.

Basic Techniques
TIDAL WIND

It is a fact, that any time we are sailing in tide or current, the wind that is being experienced will have been modified by the stream.

Consider the first diagram. It can be seen quite clearly that on a flat calm day, when there is a strong current, there will be a tidal wind when the yacht is drifting free.

It is only a small progression of that same logic to see

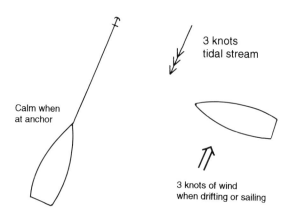

3 knots
tidal stream

Calm when
at anchor

3 knots of wind
when drifting or sailing

that on a day such as exemplified in the second diagram, this tidal wind still exists and can be added to the true wind to give a combined vector. It is always this combined wind that we sail in, whenever there is a current or tidal stream. This means that we do not have to consider it until the current changes in direction or strength. Then, when the tidal component of the sailing wind changes, it will probably affect both the rate and direction of the sailing wind.

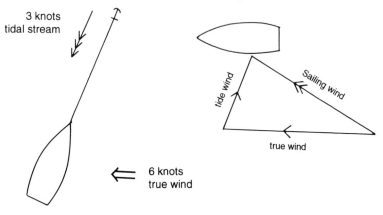

3 knots
tidal stream

tide wind

Sailing wind

true wind

6 knots
true wind

Basic Techniques
SPEED POLAR CURVES

When I first started taking a serious interest in racing navigation in the early Seventies, speed polar curves were things which few people really knew much about and which were utilised mainly on only the top America's Cup yachts. Computer technology has brought the concept right down to the average club cruiser/racer and in fact rough polar curves are even shown in most cruiser evaluation articles in yachting magazines!

For me, the turning point from speed polar curves being a nice theory — to being a reality — came with the advent of the readily available data from velocity prediction programs (VPP's). Available not only to the mega wealthy but also to the ordinary sailor. The most common use of these VPP's is within the IMS (International Measurement System) handicapping rule. This gives speed polar information for the yacht as a by-product of the rating system — but this does not devalue its use.

Back to basics for a moment. I can almost hear some of you saying — "What is a speed polar curve?". In simple terms, it is a graph for each wind speed showing how the speed differs according to apparent wind angle as shown in the diagram. It allows you to both have target speeds to aim for when there is not a competitor next to you, and also to plan ahead and look at different "what if" situations.

If you haven't and cannot get full polar information for

your yacht, you should at least try to get enough data to look at the critical parts of the speed polar curve, namely the gybing angles downwind for maximum v.m.g. and the corresponding points upwind.

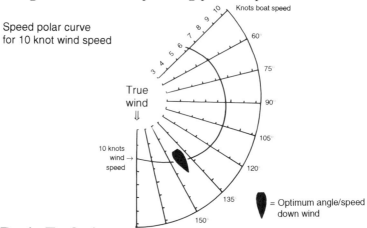

Speed polar curve
for 10 knot wind speed

Basic Techniques
FINISHING LINE BIAS

Assuming that the finish is at the end of the last beat, then the favoured end will be the DOWNWIND end. This is merely a mirror image of the situation at the start line.

If the starting and finishing lines are one and the same, then you should know the bearing of the line and will therefore be able to work out the favoured end by comparison of the line bearing and the wind direction.

Similarly, if at any time during the race, for example at the end of a round of the course, you pass through the finishing line, it makes sense to take a bearing of the line for the same purpose.

The difficulty comes when the finishing line is laid as you approach it. Then you will have no directional information to plan with. If the committee is following the best systems, they should have laid the line perpendicular to the last leg, but it is rare to be able to rely on this. You must therefore practice looking at a line from a position to leeward and then judge which end is further to leeward.

Instruments and Electronics
THE ESSENTIALS

"What are the essential instruments?"; "Do I need a v.m.g. meter?"; "Should we have an on-deck computer linked to the instruments?".

These are some of the recent questions I have been asked when coaching various racing yachts and cruiser racers. In most cases my answer has been the same — concentrate on the basics before getting into the huge expense of instruments which may even hinder your performance.

In my opinion, the essentials needed to race effectively in most situations are a good compass, tell-tales on all the genoas and the leech of the mainsail, accurate boat-speed information and an echo sounder if racing near shoal water. Anything else is a luxury and the difference in performance between having or not having more sophisticated instruments is going to be marginal. Sure, once you have bought the new sails, faired the keel and rudder and learnt how to get the best out of your yacht and these basics — it DOES make a difference to have more sophisticated instrumentation.

The problem is one of priorities; both of money and time. Few yachts have unlimited budgets, so any money spent on instruments means less spent on essential like sails and rigging. From the time point of view, over-complicated instrumentation often distracts the navigator from genuinely important tasks. He may be seduced into using the machines for their own sake, to the detriment of good basic work.

Instruments and Electronics
THE DANGERS OF V.M.G.

One of the most over-rated displays on an instrument system is the v.m.g. (velocity made good) meter. This shows how the compromise between pointing angle and speed is working out, either up or down wind.

As a tuning or trimming aid, a v.m.g. readout is quite useful so long as the boatspeed, windspeed and wind direction information is reasonably well calibrated. However, as a helmsman's aid the instrument should be banned from his sight (together with the echo sounder!).

Assume that you are going upwind at (say) 6 knots and the v.m.g. is averaging about 4.8 knots. You can get an immediate and huge increase in v.m.g. at any time by simply pointing further into the wind — the angle decreases but in the short term the boatspeed will stay the same. Once the boatspeed starts to drop however, it is impossible to get the v.m.g. to pick up again quickly, since once again the inertia of the yacht prevents it accelerating immediately one bears away, so this just further reduces v.m.g. in the short term. The same sort of problem is also experienced going downwind.

If kept away from the helmsman and used by the trimmers over an average of 30 seconds or so, they can gradually optimise the trim to make the helmsman actually sail to the best v.m.g. They can try sheeting in a touch, so that the helmsman who is sailing on the tell-tales has to point higher. Then, after a period of time to allow the speed to stabilise again, the trimmers can see if this has given a better v.m.g. So to recap, a useful trimming tool — but don't let the helmsman see it!

Instruments and Electronics
CALIBRATION
However simple or sophisticated your instruments may be, they are of limited use unless they are calibrated.

With simple, unlinked systems which give raw data, this is not too critical since you can get to know what boatspeed you normally sail to, even if the number has little to do with reality. For example; one well-known class of 33 footers in the UK normally have a simple set of instruments fitted and most of the fleet think that they sail upwind at over 7 knots with a v.m.g. approaching 6 knots. In reality a good IOR One Tonner would have difficulty achieving numbers like those, but it doesn't really matter if you are racing one-design.

Once you have instruments which collect data from more than one source and link the data to give a secondary function, calibration becomes much more critical. Take a simple example such as true wind angle off the bow. This combines apparent wind angle with apparent wind speed and boat speed to give the new value and any errors in the basic functions can be magnified (or reduced) in the linked data. This means that the data from the combined sources is unreliable, probably in an unforecastable way.

The message is, calibrate your instruments, especially if they link different functions together.

Instruments and Electronics
THE EFFECT OF WIND SHEAR

As discussed on page 122, wind shear can have a big effect on wind direction and strength, particularly on days when there is little mixing of the lower and upper air masses. The effect normally demonstrates itself as large differences between the apparent wind angles on each tack and this in turn throws out any more complex read-outs which use that basic data.

With real sophistication, it is possible to handle wind shear on a moment by moment basis to effectively remove it from your calculations (see Mark Chisnell's book in this series for more detailed information). However, in my opinion, the most important thing is to be able to recognise the effect when it happens because it can be quite off-putting. Magnetic wind direction, v.m.g, the look of the sails and lots beside can all look wrong and then it is all too easy for the crew to say that the instruments are unreliable. They may then never rely on those bits of data which are still accurate — and all because of the effect of wind shear.

To give an extreme example of how wind shear can affect you, I did a S.O.R.C. series in Florida on the One Tonner Jade back in 1985. One of the races took the fleet out of Tampa Bay and then to a buoy about 60 miles down the coast. In the One Ton section of the fleet we had a beat all the way there and a square run all the way back. Our instruments were going haywire with the wind direction showing as a reach in both directions. What we did not realise until after the race, was that the larger yachts in the fleet actually sailed down the coast on a starboard beam reach with only the top third of their sails working and the lower parts flapping, then returned on a port tack reach. On this occasion, it appears that there was a totally different wind from about 35 feet above sea level which we could record but not use. Needless to say, the One Tonners did not do very well in that race!

Instruments and Electronics
KEEP YOUR OWN WAYPOINT INFORMATION
Until everyone is sailing with a GPS navigator on board, most racing boats will be kitted out with either Decca or Loran-C, depending on their locality. With both of these systems, the absolute accuracy is not too good but the repeatability is significantly better. This means that once you have been to a buoy or headland once, the position readout will be the same every other

time you return there. This is due to the fixed errors which are part of both systems.

So, if you go round a mark that you are going to use again in the future, it is wise to record the latitude and longitude given by your Decca or Loran. If you compare this with the actual position as on the chart, you will get a good idea of the local accuracy of the fix. The nice thing is, that it does not matter whether you use the same set next time or not, it is the system which introduces the errors and not the set.

I keep a little black book with the actual and recorded positions of most marks that I have been round and carry it with me whenever I am sailing on a new boat. In fog, an error of ¼ mile can mean the difference between rounding the mark and not even seeing it.

Instruments and Electronics
DO NOT RELY TOTALLY ON
ELECTRONIC NAVAIDS
I started out as a navigator in the days before Decca, let alone GPS and I still maintain enough information to keep a basic estimated position going. On too many racing yachts, the advent of the silicon chip as a position fixer has meant that the "navigators" are not much more than good computer operators. Even those who have the knowledge to keep an E.P. going rarely do so, relying totally on the "green light" from the electronics to tell them their position.

My philosophy is that I am:
— a) lazy — and b) cautious. The former means that I

am reluctant to do any work which I consider unnecessary, while the second point means that I have seen too many electronic boxes fail at critical moments to put my absolute faith in them.

When sailing offshore, I use the Decca or Loran all the time and by and large find them both reliable and accurate. My caution makes me do two simple things, both of which have stood me in good stead on more than one occasion. The first and most important is that I write down my position (from the navaid) every so often, normally every half hour or so and maintain a reasonable log to show my course, speed etc. alongside these regular positions. This means that if at some time during the race, the Decca ceases to give a green light, I am not lost and have only a small amount of "proper" navigation to do before I once again know my position.

The second way that I exercise caution (especially with Decca, which might jump lanes) is to compare the electronically produced position with a very rough E.P. based on course steered and distance travelled since the last good electronic fix and an approximate set and drift for the current. If the electronic position is within spitting distance of my E.P. then I accept it without further question, if there is a discrepancy, I think hard before accepting either position.

Crew-Work _____

Preparation
SPINNAKER PACKING — METHOD 1
SIMPLE

Spinnakers can be packed in many different ways, but whatever method you choose they all have the same basic requirements — that is to enable the spinnaker to be hoisted easily and without twists.

With small and/or lightweight spinnakers, the packing can be simple and need take very little time. The principle is to find the head and then work down one luff to the clew, roughly flaking the luff tape as you go and keeping it in hand. In theory, this should ensure that the sail is not twisted and it could be put into its turtle or bag.

In practice, I like to refine this slightly and work down both luffs unless the sail is tiny. To facilitate this, I start at the head and attach this to a purpose fitted hook fixed somewhere high up in the working area below deck. (Coat hooks or a carbine hook are ideal, and it is useful to fix one on each side so that you can always work on the windward side.) Work down one luff to the clew and then hang up that clew before working down the second luff tape and hanging up the other clew. At this stage, you have the whole sail in front of you, untwisted and with all three corners available. The middle of the spinnaker can be stuffed into the bag with the three corners going in last.

Preparation
SPINNAKER PACKING — METHOD 2
IN STOPS

The simple packing *method 1* works well and ensures that the sail is not twisted, but it is not always easy to hoist the sail once it has been stuffed into the bag in that manner. Often the top part of the sail will be buried under lower sections and this makes it hard to drag it out of the bag with the halyard. Therefore for larger spinnakers a somewhat more refined method of packing is required.

On large yachts, the heavier spinnakers will be packed in stops so that they can be hoisted to the top before the are broken out. Normally rubber bands are used to hold the spinnaker together in a tube-like shape but really large spinnakers should be stopped into a "star" shape. The top half of the sail will be made into one tube and each clew will be stopped separately in order to allow the windward corner to be taken to the pole end and the pole pre-set before the hoist.

Whether it is going to be stopped simply, just from the head down, or in three stages, the principle is the same. The spinnaker is passed through a bucket with no bottom, onto which rubber bands will have been stretched beforehand and these are applied every metre or so from the head downwards. A tip when using an ordinary bucket for the job, is to tape a batten down one side of the bucket as this makes it much easier to lift the bands. The bucket should have two ties at its top rim to enable it to be tied to a convenient place below. The spinnaker can then be pulled through it without having to hang onto the bucket at all.

Normally, stops will be applied about ⅔ of the way down the sail and the foot will be left unstopped. In this case, two or three bands should be applied wherever the stops finish so that the spinnaker does not break out too easily while it is being hoisted.

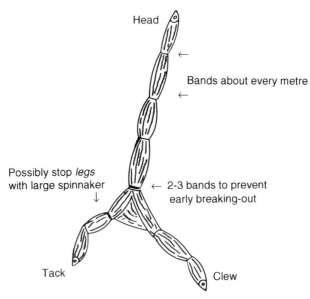

Preparation
IDENTIFYING THE HALYARDS
The halyards must be easily identifiable at all times. This means that halyard mast exits should be labelled but much more important is colour coding. Modern rope materials allow good coding by colour and this should always be utilised.

Nautor who build Swan yachts, used to have a policy

that all Swan halyards were white and all their sheets were either white or white with blue flecks regardless of what the owner wanted. Their attitude seemed to be that the only colour coordination requirement should be to match the traditional white hull and blue line down the coachroof. Whether this policy is still in existence I am not sure but I have noticed that more and more Swans (who generally have the most traditional of all cruiser/racer owners) are changing to colour coding their ropes to facilitate easier crew work. If the concept is filtering down to this bastion of good taste, then it must be acceptable to the rest of us with "lesser" yachts!

If the halyards are all rope, then the rope colour itself can act as sufficient identification. With wire/rope combinations each halyard should have a coloured parrel ball on the end by the snap shackle to allow for easy visual identification on the foredeck and to prevent the splice being wound into the sheave at the masthead. Ideally, the port halyard should have a red ball, the starboard a green one and a central genoa halyard could have a blue or black ball. It makes life even easier,especially in the cockpit, if the same colour coding is carried through to the colours of the rope tails.

Preparation
KEEPING HALYARDS UNTWISTED
Even if our halyards are neatly colour coded, it is still all too easy to end up with them twisted at the top of the mast so that they either chafe against each other or jam with a sail half up. It is up to the bow man or

mast man to ensure that they stay untwisted and sensible stowage will help his task.

During the day it is not too difficult, he can look aloft every time a new halyard is used to ensure that it is not twisted and if it is, then the situation can be rectified before the halyard is actually used.

At night the whole job becomes harder. Even with very good torches it is incredibly difficult to really see what is happening to the halyards at the top of the mast and in any case it is desirable to restrict the use of torches as much as possible. Therefore, the stowage of the halyards at the base of the mast becomes even more critical.

In basic terms, it should be possible to unclip any halyard from its stowage and know, without needing to look aloft that it can be taken forward and used with impunity. This means that the halyards should never be jammed together or clipped onto one ring as it is too easy to accidentally twist them. On larger yachts it may be possible to have a purpose built, stainless wire cage fitted with dividers to keep the snap shackles apart. On smaller yachts it is worth clipping the port spinnaker halyard to the port shroud base, the genoa halyard amidships and the starboard spinnaker halyard to the starboard shroud base. This keeps them apart and easily identifiable.

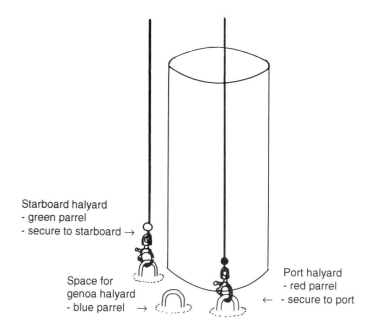

Starboard halyard
- green parrel
- secure to starboard →

Space for
genoa halyard
- blue parrel →

Port halyard
- red parrel
← - secure to port

Preparation
LABEL THE HALYARD CLUTCHES

On most racing yachts nowadays there is a tendency to reduce both weight and cost by cutting down the number of cabin top winches and replacing them with more and more stoppers or clutches. This makes very good sense but can lead to confusion when trying to identify a particular rope.

Most yachts go to the extent of labelling the handles of each clutch to identify it's purpose but a useful tip is to label the underside of the handles as well as the tops. This means that you will still be able to tell what is what, even when the clutches are open.

Preparation
LEAD THE TRIPPING LINE FORWARD

When sailing a yacht which gybes using the dip pole method, it is possible to reduce crewing problems by allowing the bowman to trip the guy out of the spinnaker pole himself, rather than having the mast man do the trip.

On most poles the trip line is led inside the pole to the inboard end so that it exits very near the mast. If this line is then led through a small block which is secured near the centre of the pole and a sail tie is attached to it, the bowman should be able to both trip the pole and swing it in to himself using this sail tie. This will leave the mast man free to concentrate on the pole uphaul.

Preparation
CLEATS FOR UPHAUL AND
SPINNAKER HALYARDS AT MAST

If you sail on a yacht where there often seem to be too few people to do the necessary jobs during spinnaker hoists and gybes, the addition of a couple of halyard clutches can reduce the crew required by at least one person.

The spinnaker pole uphaul (topping lift) should be led from its mast exit to the cleat or stopper near the cockpit VIA an open cleat on the mast. If one of the aluminium "Clam Cleats" with a spring loaded cover is used then the uphaul can be cleated at the mast whenever necessary or the cleat can be ignored for general pole adjustments. The advantage of this system is that the mast man is able to raise and lower the pole during a gybe with no help from anyone else and without the inevitable friction losses inherent in systems where the job is done from the cockpit. In my experience on yachts which only have one cleat aft, it will normally be necessary either to winch the pole up (which is very slow) or have a second person bouncing the topping lift at the mast.

A similar situation exists for the spinnaker halyard. During spinnaker hoists you often see the mast man actually pulling the halyard up, but with a second crew member tailing the halyard back in the cockpit. If you put a halyard clutch on the mast, just below the halyard exit, you can do away with the tailer aft.

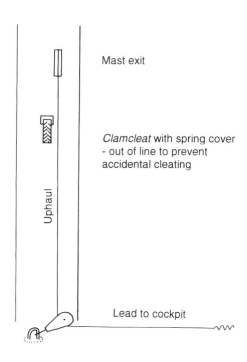

Mast exit

Clamcleat with spring cover - out of line to prevent accidental cleating

Uphaul

Lead to cockpit

Preparation
CLIP SHEETS AND GUYS TOGETHER

My preferred method of rigging the sheets and guys is first to clip each guy to its appropriate sheet and then to clip the two sheets together. When clipping the sheets together, do it so that one snap shackle is free so that this can be attached to the sail before unclipping the sheets from each other.

The advantage of clipping the guys onto the sheets and not vice versa is that it enables you to remove the lazy guy easily when the wind drops light. The reason for clipping the two pairs of ropes together in the first place is to allow the gear to be moved to whichever side it is required without anyone going forward.

Preparation
HOW TO CLIP GENOA SHEETS TOGETHER

Assuming that your genoa sheets have J-locks or similar specialised snap shackles spliced to them, when clipping the sheets together while they are not in use, it is best to clip one snap shackle around the rope part of the other sheet rather than clipping the two shackles together. This means that when you want to attach them to the sail you can do it without unclipping the sheets from each other and having to hold one rope in your teeth.

Preparation
MARKING THE GENOA LUFF

While it is important to mark the halyards themselves so that you can see how near to full hoist you are and to have reference points for the halyard man to work to, these are not always easy to see. A more easily visible mark is also useful.

One way to have reference marks which are clearly visible is to put a large mark on the luff of each genoa, somewhere near the lower tell-tale position and then to mark the headstay with three or four evenly spaced lines at the same height. As the halyard is tightened, so the mark on the genoa luff will rise relative to the marks on the headstay, thus giving a clear indication of the amount of luff tension. A similar system can be employed on the mast and mainsail.

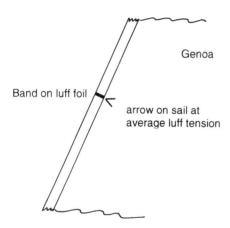

Foredeck
SPINNAKER SET UP IN ROUGH WATER
There will inevitably be occasions when you are about to bear away around the windward mark and set the spinnaker (bear-away set) and you are forced onto the lay-line too early. If the conditions are rough this often results in the spinnaker being washed out of its bag before you are ready to hoist.

On small yachts, you can avoid this problem by hoisting from much further back in the boat, maybe from the main hatch as in J-24s, but on larger yachts you are virtually forced to hoist from the foredeck.

Although it is normal to set the spinnaker up and to hoist from the leeward side, there is no compelling reason for this and it is quite possible to prepare and hoist the spinnaker from the windward side of the foredeck. All you need to do is get the sheets, guys and halyards around to the leeward side as usual, but then clip the bag onto the windward side of the foredeck. Next bring the sheets, guys and halyard under the foot of the genoa, under the spinnaker pole and up to the spinnaker itself before clipping them on.

When the hoist occurs, the spinnaker will be pulled across the foredeck and under the genoa foot before going up, but this should not normally present any problems.

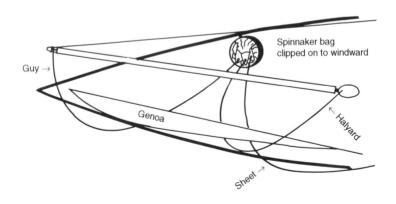

74

Foredeck
GUY-RUN
SPINNAKER DROP

When I first started offshore racing, the snap shackles in use were fairly basic and if the spinnaker sheet was allowed to flog then invariably they shook off. Nowadays technology has marched on and most yachts sail with good quality snap shackles which will stay attached in most situations until you decide to trip them away.

So far as the effect this progress has had on spinnaker drops, it is worth looking back a few years to a race I did as skipper on a Nicholson 33 called *Griffin*. This yacht was typical of her era, with a small mainsail, huge fore-triangle and heavily pinched ends which made her virtually uncontrollable downwind in a blow. I had been asleep below for an hour or so, when I was woken by first one then another violent broach and upon going on deck it became obvious that it was well past time to drop the spinnaker in the rising wind. My crew were trainees who had only had a week in the Solent, in flat water and force two to three winds, so when I suggested to my bowman that he should go up to the foredeck and trip the spinnaker away from the guy, he quite reasonably told me that he would rather watch me do it myself — those weren't the words he used but that was what he meant! I briefed the crew that the guy should be eased, the downhaul kept tight and that I would trip the guy as soon as I could reach it and forward I went. As the pole went forward, the downhaul wasn't kept quite tight enough and so the spinnaker flew further and further from the pole end. This, combined with my weight on the foredeck made the already difficult to handle boat totally impossible and we broached again. As I stood on the pulpit, up to my armpits in rushing water, in the middle of the night, I decided that there must be a better way to drop the spinnaker than this!!

With good snap shackles on the sheets and guys there is no longer any need for "heroism" of the type described above. My standard method of dropping now is to let the guy run until the pole hits the forestay and the spinnaker collapses behind the genoa. At this moment the guy is temporarily held and the halyard is let go completely, the spinnaker is pulled into the main hatch by working up the leech and finally the guy is let go and the foot is pulled in. At no time until the spinnaker is down does anyone need to go forward and there is no danger of broaching or losing control.

Foredeck
WHAT TYPE OF
SNAP SHACKLE?

Having described the guy-run spinnaker drop in the section above, mention was made of good snap shackles, but what sort should be used?

In my opinion the best general type for any situation where the rope may flog is one of the triggerlatch type which need a spike to release them. There are various makes, Barient Sparcraft brought out the first of this type but now Lewmar, Gibb and others make broadly similar designs.

If you are stuck with plunger type snap shackles on the yacht you sail aboard, then in most cases they will have lengths of string tied to the plunger to make release easier. My advice is to cut this off the snap shackles attached to all sheets and guys to prevent the inevitable accidental release when the string gets caught on the forestay or guard-rail.

Foredeck
DOUBLE SHEETS AND GUYS
If doing dip pole gybes then double sheets and guys will be the norm, but on many smaller yachts who gybe by end-for-ending the pole, only single sheets will be used.

In my opinion, double sheets and guys should always be used for gybing on all boats over about 8 metres except in light airs. Having a lazy guy enables the load to be taken on both sheets just prior to the gybe so that the pole can be released from the mast without any danger of it being catapulted backwards by a loaded guy. It also means that the new guy can easily be put into the pole end and the pole re-attached to the mast once again, without having to fight excessive loads.

I have sailed on quite small boats like J-24s often enough to have seen the force sometimes needed by the mast man (and his assistant?), to realise that lazy guys are really necessary as soon as the spinnaker size increases.

Foredeck
GYBE-SET: TOPPING LIFT POSITION

In any gybe-set one of the problems is that there will inevitably be a delay before the pole can be lifted. If you set the pole topping lift in the traditional manner it will be inside the genoa sheets to allow the genoa to gybe across. This means that even when the genoa has been gybed, you will need to pull in a lot of slack from the pole lift, which wastes time. More importantly, you will need to lift the genoa sheet a long way to get it both above the pole and right at the front end of the pole, forward of the lift.

If you re-rig the pole topping lift so that it exits from the mast fairly close to the hounds, it will be possible to rig it onto the pole outside both the genoa and genoa sheets. This then means that as soon as the genoa starts to go across in the gybe, the pole lift can be tensioned and this in turn will immediately start to raise the pole.

Foredeck
SET UP THE SPINNAKER IN GOOD TIME

During most races you will be able to anticipate on which gybe you will be setting the spinnaker, long before you reach the lay line for the windward mark. In these cases it is nearly always most sensible to set up the spinnaker and its gear in three stages.

The spinnaker bag should be clipped onto what will become the leeward side when this side is to windward, that is normally one tack before the lay line. The pole should not be raised until approaching the mark on the final tack, when it too will be to windward. This ensures that you have bodies on the leeward side of the foredeck for as short a time as possible.

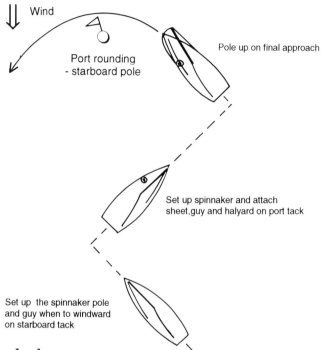

Wind

Port rounding - starboard pole

Pole up on final approach

Set up spinnaker and attach sheet,guy and halyard on port tack

Set up the spinnaker pole and guy when to windward on starboard tack

Foredeck
GETTING A SPARE HALYARD OVER THE POLE

There are many occasions when the spinnaker is up and you need to get a spare halyard from one side of the pole to the other. It is possible to practice rope throwing and risk heaving the halyard up and over the pole but whenever I try to do this, the end of the halyard always ends up falling between the pole end and the pole lift, thus causing even more problems.

Assuming that you normally sail with the genoa sheets over the pole, a much easier way to get a spare halyard over the pole end is to use these genoa sheets. Pull as much slack genoa sheet as needed to the side where the halyard is currently, tie a loose loop in the sheet and clip the halyard to this loop. Then all you need to do is pull the genoa sheet across to the other side and the halyard will have to come with it. Don't forget to untie the loop from the genoa sheet!

Cockpit
TAILING TO WINDWARD
During a tack it is important to get crew weight onto the new windward side as soon as possible. One person who usually stays to leeward until the genoa has been fully wound in, is the genoa sheet tailer. However, on most yachts it is possible for the tailer to get hold of the new sheet and immediately take it across the yacht to the high side, using his body movement to bring in the slack. From here he can tail the last metre or so properly before swinging his legs over the side.

Cockpit
RIDING TURNS ON A WINCH
However careful you are as a crew, there will be the odd occasions when a riding turn happens. The most important thing to do is to consider the immediate implications and overcome these, rather than worry too much about clearing the winch straight away.

For example, just after a tack the rider is most likely to happen with the sheet still needing to be wound in by a few centimetres. In this situation it is nearly always possible to continue to wind in the sheet without stopping, then get rid of the riding turns later.

There are three basic ways of undoing riding turns and which method is most appropriate will depend on the situation.

1) Cut the rope. This is a total panic measure which should only be used in really extreme cases, for example where you must tack to avoid rocks or another yacht! Consider both the cost and the hassle of needing a replacement rope. Having said that, it is sometimes necessary and all crew members should know the whereabouts of a knife.

2) Take the load off the offending rope. In a many circumstances it will be possible to rig a spare line as a temporary replacement, either using a rolling hitch on the sheet itself or by attaching a new rope to the sail. If this spare line can then be fully loaded the pressure should come off the rope with the riding turns, which can then be removed from the winch.

3) Remove one riding turn at a time. If the turns are really well jammed, then it may not be possible to remove them easily, even with the load removed from the rope. The best system to employ in this case will be to take the tail of the rope THE WRONG WAY round the jammed winch, lead it to another winch and literally winch each riding turn out. Once one turn has been removed you can take the tail the wrong way

round the winch again and remove the next turn, and so on.

Cockpit
GYBE-SET: SHEETING THE GENOA

Over the years I have watched many spinnaker gybe-sets get messed up, normally for the same reason.

In most cases, it is felt that whatever yacht you are sailing on, there are never quite enough crew members to cope with the gybe-set and therefore some tasks get either left completely or at best they get half done.

One such task is the genoa sheeting. Because you are hoisting the spinnaker, it is often thought that the genoa does not matter, so it does not get sheeted in properly on the new side. However, although it is true to say that you are not interested in the genoa itself, it is far from true that the sheeting does not matter. Unless the genoa is sheeted in properly during the gybe it will inevitably go forward and wrap itself around the spinnaker clew, thus preventing the spinnaker from being set.

Cockpit
GYBE-SET: GUY ON TOO SOON

Apart from any other mistakes during a gybe-set, one of the most common is for the person on the guy to try to get it on too soon during the manoeuvre.

Unless the pole is at least above the level of the guard-rails before the guy is loaded, it will be impossible to raise it at all, due to the downward pull of the guy. It is just a matter of timing and awareness, if you are on the guy, watch forward and hesitate before pulling on it.

Cockpit
MAKE UP THE NEW WINCH

Whenever you are going upwind, the lazy genoa sheet should always be made up onto its winch in preparation for the next tack. Two or three turns round the winch and a handle somewhere nearby means that you are able to crash tack with reasonable efficiency. As soon as a tack has been completed, get ready for the next one!

General
SLEEPING ON THE SIDE DECK

On modern racing yachts it is very important to keep the crew sitting as hard out as possible whenever going upwind in anything other than light airs. In an offshore race this means that a really keen crew will, by and large, sleep on the rail. There are exceptions, in very cold weather or on exceptionally long races it may not be feasible. Also if the beat is very long then it is often best to have a rota of at least one or two crew at a time going below to sleep properly. However these exceptions still leave the majority of the crew sitting on the rail and trying to get to sleep. This is definitely an acquired art and a dubious pleasure, but it does make the yacht go faster!

There are a few "musts" if the crew are going to get any useful sleep at all. To start with they must feel secure. The rules help here in allowing crew to put their heads under the top guard-rail while insisting that they stay inside the lower rail. This means that you can wedge yourself in — so long as the lines don't break. The crew must believe that the guard-rails and stanchions are strong enough or they will spend the night hours thinking about the consequences of the lower rail parting! Inshore it is accepted practice to loosen the lower guard-rail a little so that the crew can hike out a bit further. Offshore it is important not to have the lines slack enough so that anyone could slide out. To this end I like to have discontinuous guard-lines, attached at each of the aft two or three stanchions. This stops the nasty habit of the rail going very tight when someone heavy hikes out hard the other side of the next stanchion and then going really slack when he moves in again.

Although a lot of racing crews dislike wearing safety harnesses because of the supposed restrictions they put on rapid movement around the boat, I believe that in most situations you will sleep much more readily if you know that you are attached to the boat — so I normally wear a harness when trying to sleep, especially at night.

Comfort is the next priority after security. A 30mm toe-rail cutting into the back of your legs does not help sleep, nor does the shock of the occasional wave breaking over your face. It is possible to buy oilskin trousers with padded thighs to get over the toe-rail problem, or the crew can sit on a folded dacron sail. Alternatively, unless the class rules prevent it, consider cutting the toe-rail away over the area where the crew sit. Good quality oilskins with a hood which can be drawn over most of your face almost completes the picture. One other consideration is that sitting still, possibly for hours at a time can be very cold, so warm clothing is essential and I find a thermal long john most comfortable, except in very warm weather.

General
CREW WEIGHT IN LIGHT AIRS

In earlier sections it has already been stressed that the position of your crew weight is vital to good performance but for most people this chiefly means sitting out hard when going upwind in a breeze. In light airs and particularly in sloppy seas, it can be just as important to concentrate the crew weight as low and as centrally as possible.

As a general principle, this means that the crew should always be encouraged to sit rather than stand and to keep their weight out of the ends of the boat in light airs. If going upwind in these conditions then you may sit most of the crew on the leeward side deck to get her heeling to leeward and allowing gravity to help the sails fill. Downwind most boats will merely get their crew to sit near the middle but in fact there is often a big advantage in getting anyone who is not needed on deck to sit below, with their weight directly over the keel.

General
CO-ORDINATION
CLOSE REACHING IN A BLOW

Close co-ordination between the helmsman, the trimmers and the rest of the crew is normally required if
you are going to close reach successfully on a windy or
gusty day.

As a gust hits the boat, the apparent wind angle will
move aft because the boat is unable to accelerate
immediately (see Section 2, apparent wind vectors). If
nothing is done to adjust the sails, this will result in
them stalling out, thus generating more side force
than forward drive and therefore making the
yacht heel more. The increase in wind strength will
also increase the heeling forces and this in turn
will increase the weather helm. Unless handled
properly, the combination of forces described above
will result in the yacht screwing up to windward in a
broach whenever a gust hits, rather than utilising
the increase in available power and accelerating
away.

Because the apparent wind angle will automatically
move aft in a gust while on a close reach, it is
important to be ready to square the pole, ease the
spinnaker sheet and ease the mainsail as the gust hits
(or just before it arrives). This will keep the sails set
correctly and may be all that is necessary to keep the
yacht tracking straight and going fast. As the power
comes on, there will inevitably be an increase in
weather helm and the helmsman must be ready to
counter this with the tiller or wheel.

If the gust is particularly strong, some de-powering may be needed to keep the weather helm within controllable limits. In this case the yacht should be de-powered from the back first. As well as letting the mainsheet out, the boom vang should be dumped to remove leech tension from the mainsail. Any available crew should hike out as hard as possible and anyone who was to leeward should have moved to the high side. If the rudder stalls because of the big rudder angle needed to keep in a straight line, the helmsman should be ready to momentarily straighten the tiller, thus allowing water to flow over the rudder again before once more attempting to make the yacht bear away.

At this stage it is likely that control will have been maintained and the yacht should have picked up speed, thus drawing the apparent wind forward again. The spinnaker should be trimmed on edge and as control is regained the helmsman can gently head back up to course and power can be returned to the mainsail.

Once the gust is over, the reverse situation will apply. The apparent wind will move forward and it will be possible to sail higher while maintaining speed and without undue heel. Sails should be trimmed in, the spinnaker guy eased forward a little and a somewhat higher course sailed.

Close spinnaker reaching on a gusty day should be hard work for all the crew; guy back, ease sheet is immediately followed by guy forward, sheet in — but it should also be an exhilarating and fast point of sail.

General
GOING UP THE MAST

Two things make going up a mast at sea easier. The first is a good climbing type harness (Lirakis or similar). This will allow you to half climb/half be hoisted, rather than having to sit passively in a standard bosun's chair.

The other and even more important consideration, is to make sure that you always go up the windward side regardless of which side of the rig you need to work at when aloft.

However you go up, it is vital that you hold on really tight. The forces acting on your body to swing you away from the mast are quite astonishing when near the top of a tall rig in a seaway. If possible have a harness clipped to a spare halyard or to a shroud to stop you swinging too far.

Helming
FEATHERING
TO KEEP HER ON HER FEET IN A GUST

When sailing upwind there will be times when you get hit by a gust and are overpowered. There are two ways to get over this problem.

One way is to ask for the traveller to be eased down the track and possibly even ease the mainsheet in extreme gusts. This will keep the boat sailing but it will inevitably lose ground to windward since the yacht will tend to sag off a few degrees. This will be a good system to utilise in choppy water when you need to keep the power on to get through the waves.

The alternative that is often more effective, especially in smooth water, is to feather the yacht into the wind while keeping the mainsail hard in. If delicately done this should keep the heel angle reasonable while also maintaining a good pointing angle. Since you do not need much power in smooth water this method will not lose much speed either, therefore your vmg. will be better than if you dump the traveller.

In extremely gusty conditions or at times when there are some waves, a compromise between the two methods is normally the best approach — ease the traveller a little and feather slightly.

Helming
AVOIDING THE ROLLING CRAZIES

Running square in a strong wind is one of the hardest helming jobs. As seen in Spinnaker-Trim for a windy run (page 115), the sail trim is important to reduce the roll, but overdoing sail trim will normally reduce the available power and will make the boat slower, even if under control. A good downwind helmsman should be able to control the yacht in most conditions without having to resort to excessive de-powering of the rig.

If the yacht is rolling a little but is not in any danger of going out of control, then nothing needs to be done. Either over-trimming the sails or unnecessary rudder movement will only slow the boat down. When the rolling becomes uncomfortable and the helmsman starts to feel that he may soon lose control, this is when he must start to steer to limit the roll.

In basic terms, the concept is very simple. Whichever way the top of the mast is rolling, the hull must move the same way in order to keep the yacht upright. The problem is that while the boat can roll quite quickly in response to a gust or wave, the hull has considerable mass and therefore takes time to respond to a rudder movement. This means that the helmsman needs to antiipate each roll and start to correct it before it has started which takes timing and practice. If the boat is already rolling rhythmically then the helm needs to be put over for a starboard turn even while the yacht is still rolling to port. This way, once the masthead has moved through its arc to starboard again the hull is already under it.

In waves the difficulties are exacerbated by each wave coming past the yacht, causing additional rolling. Once again the helmsman must anticipate how the yacht is going to react to the wave and start applying gentle rudder correction BEFORE the yacht is veered off course.

Helming
HELMING UPWIND
IN WAVES

The main object when helming upwind in waves should be to keep the bow in the water as much as possible. Once the bow lifts out, it will almost inevitably slam to some extent when it returns to its rightful medium and this will always slow the yacht. The other criteria is to keep pointing as high as possible without losing boatspeed — that is maintaining a high vmg. at all times.

In practice, this will mean pointing into the wind while going up the wave and bearing away down the back of the wave (see also page 120). This sounds simple and in truth it is not difficult specially in large or regular waves. In smaller waves however, we experience the same problem of inertia and a time lag between moving the rudder and the yacht responding that was talked about in the previous tip. The bear away over the crest of the wave, is the most critical part of the manoeuvre since if this is not right then the yacht will come out of the wave still pointing into the wind and in extreme cases the majority of the hull may be flying. As the yacht goes up the face of the wave, the helm needs to be applied to initiate the bear away so that by the time the crest is reached, the yacht is already responding to the rudder and is bearing away.

In my experience, if you find that the yacht is out of synch with the waves, it is slower to attempt to play the wave than it is just to steer straight. So if you find the yacht slamming over a particular few waves, bear away slightly to regain speed and ignore the waves for a few moments until you can get back in tune with their pattern.

In any event it is vital that the helmsman can see the waves as they approach the yacht and particularly with a wheel I often find it best to steer on heel angle and boatspeed when in waves rather than trying to keep the tell-tales working all the time.

Helming
TOO NARROW A GROOVE?

If you find that it is impossible or very difficult to keep the yacht "in the groove" when sailing upwind and the tell-tales always seem to be either flapping or stalled then you need to get the trimmer to re-trim the genoa.

There are several possible reasons for this phenomenon although they all boil down to the same basic point. The re-trimming options which you have are —

1) If the sail is sheeted really hard in, ease the genoa sheet a touch.
2) If the front third of the sail is very flat, make the entry more rounded by increasing halyard tension a little.
3) If the yacht is underpowered with the current sail plan, make the whole genoa fuller by easing forestay tension (ease backstay on a masthead yacht, ease runner on a fractional rig).

All of these options will mean that in theory you are unable to point quite so high to the wind since you will be altering the angle of the leading edge of the sail. In practice, if the change allows you to keep the yacht sailing nicely in the groove, then this will easily outweigh any minor disadvantage.

Whichever option you chose, don't overdo it, specially the sheet easing option or you will find that other problems start to materialise such as needing to re-adjust the sheet lead position.

Helming
ARE YOU SITTING COMFORTABLY . . .?
On yachts with tiller steering it is often really important to position yourself so that you are able to steer effectively.

One of the classic cases when this is true, is during a heavy airs gybe when most helmsmen seem to like sitting facing the sail as they go into the gybe, but who have great difficulties after the gybe, often broaching or otherwise losing control.

If you are coming into a gybe, then I recommend changing sides BEFORE the gybe. This makes steering slightly awkward for a few moments but it leaves you ideally positioned to resist the forces imposed on the rudder during the gybe itself.

Sail-Trim _____

Rig Tuning
MAST UPRIGHT?

It may seem obvious, but it is essential that the mast is set-up to be absolutely vertical to the yacht's hull. If this is not done, two things will occur. Firstly you will have different sheeting positions for either tack, or secondly, you will find that you have a boatspeed advantage on one tack over the other.

The way that most crews attempt to ascertain if the mast is vertical, is to take the main halyard down to the toe-rail on each side deck and then to see if it measures equally. This method has the disadvantage that the main halyard is so long, compared to the beam of the boat, that any differences are hard to measure because of the very small angle differences. On many production yachts the toe-rails themselves are not necessarily attached symmetrically and also remember that the main halyard sheave is often off-set at the mast-head.

A far more accurate method is to use a steel tape measure, starting from a position on the mast at about lower spreader height, down to the shroud chain plates each side. This makes for better triangulation and therefore more accurate comparisons. Using the chain plates also relates the position of the mast to its rigging, which is the most significant factor.

If you are not confident that the chainplates are

accurately positioned, measure their distance from the mast at deck level.

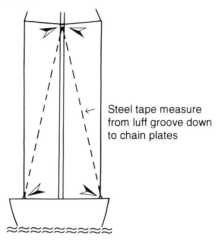

Steel tape measure
from luff groove down
to chain plates

Rig Tuning
MAST-RAKE

How much fore-and-aft mast-rake should I have? This is one of the most frequent technical questions that I am asked when coaching on cruiser racers.

As a general principle, mast-rake affects your pointing ability upwind and your ability to square run down wind. The more aft rake you have, the better you will go upwind but there will be a trade off downwind.

Mast-rake is also one of the chief factors in determining the amount of weather helm that will be experienced. Too much rake and the yacht will gripe up to windward, especially on a beat or close reach and you will be forced to depower the mainsail to compensate. Too little rake and there will be no "feel" to the helm, particularly upwind on a light day.

If you are racing a one-design yacht, the simplest way to get your rake about right, is to study one of the fast yachts in your fleet. If not, then trial and error will have to be the order of the day.

There are two basic methods of measuring mast-rake. On a calm day it is possible to take a plumb line from the back of the masthead (hoisted on the main halyard) and measure how much physical rake there is at deck level. A more reliable method and one which gives good repeatable results, is to measure the forestay length with a steel tape hoisted on the genoa halyard. Although this doesn't actually give you the rake, it is easy to measure and will allow you to reset your mast once it has been moved for any reason.

Some classes (such as the J-24 or the Sigma 38) give a maximum forestay length to stop people using more and more mast-rake. In general it is better to use the longest forestay allowed, thus giving the most allowable rake.

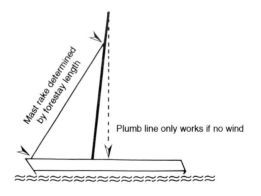

Rig Tuning
SHROUD TENSION

Most modern rigs are designed to be sailed with a mast which does not fall-off to leeward when going upwind. (That is except for the un-stayed topmast section of fractional rigs.) Once the mast starts leaning over, all sorts of detrimental things happen, so it is important to limit any lean by having the shrouds adequately tight.

On high-tech, flat-out racing yachts, the necessary shroud tension is applied by jacking-up the mast with a portable hydraulic jack and then inserting metal shims under the mast heel before the jack is removed. This is done at the outset of the racing day, well before the start. This, combined with the immensely stiff structure of such a yacht means that enormous rig tensions can be applied without breaking the boat too soon. Once racing is over for the day, the shims are removed and the tension is thus released, allowing the yacht to relax.

On the average cruiser-racer or club racing yacht, a compromise needs to be reached. The rig should be tight enough for average conditions, without being so tight that it puts unfair strains on either the yacht's hull or the mast. It is just not practicable to adjust the shroud tensions each day, nor to release them after racing, so once the shrouds have been tightened, the likelihood is that the yacht will be subjected to those loads for the rest of the season.

Having said the above, it is my experience that most

cruiser-racers sail with their rigs too slack and their performance can nearly always be improved by sensibly tightening the shrouds.

The first part of this tightening is to progressively tighten each side in turn until the rig is firm while static. Do not overdo things at this stage or you are likely to damage the threads on the turnbuckles or bottlescrews. Once the rig is secure, you should go sailing, ideally on a day when you are at the top end of being able to carry the number one genoa. Go from tack to tack, gradually tightening the LEEWARD shrouds until they only just start to go slack with the rig fully powered up. This will mean that the rig is only falling to leeward a tiny bit and any further tension will have little effect on the mast except to increase the compression strains.

Rig Tuning
PREBEND

Prebend seems to be the sort of buzz word which is not properly understood by the majority of sailors. In simple terms it describes the amount of fore-and-aft bend in the mast when the forestay is tight but without having induced any further bend with back-stay (on fractional rigs) or baby stay (on masthead boats).

The reason that prebend is good news, is that most mast sections are capable of having their middle bent forward but will kink and fail if the middle bends aft. Prebend is the easiest way of ensuring that any bend being induced due to compression loads, always goes in the safe direction. Also a mast which has safe prebend going upwind is less likely to invert when running.

The amount of prebend which is desirable will differ according to both the design of the mainsail and to the conditions at the time. Because a sail is cut with luff-round to give it shape, the more bent forward and therefore, away from the sail that the mast is, the nearer to the cut mainsail shape it becomes, and the sail therefore flattens out. In general, the more windy the conditions, the flatter the sail should be when going upwind and therefore more bend will be required. Also, the fuller the sail is cut to start with, the more bend it will be able to take before becoming completely flat.

On a medium sized, masthead yacht of about 9 metres LOA, the desired amount of prebend will be very small indeed, probably in the order of 2–3 centimeters. On a similar sized fractional rigged yacht with spreaders which are only swept back a little, the amount of prebend which is desirable for safety may increase to about 5–6 centimeters.

Apart from having to ensure that the mast bend suits the mainsail shape, it is important not to overdo prebend for two reasons. The first is that while prebend may be desirable upwind, the mast should be as straight as possible downwind to increase the power in the mainsail. Secondly, a mast is only really strong in compression while it is acting as a straight column (or nearly so). The further out of column it becomes, the easier it will be to continue bending it until ultimate failure.

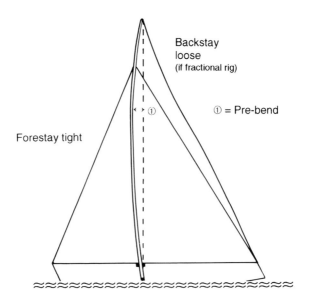

Genoa
MOVING THE GENOA FAIRLEAD
UNDER LOAD

Obviously it is very important to be able to move the genoa fairlead fore and aft while it is under load, in order to adjust the sheet lead while sailing.

On most cruiser-racers, this will mean removing the fixing pin from the car and fixing a block and tackle to the front of it. This can be attached either to an eye bolt near the front of the track or to the shroud base as convenient. If the tail is led back to the cockpit, through a rope clutch, then a cockpit winch can be used to grind the lead forward when necessary.

Except in very light winds, the lead of the sheet itself

will move the car back when the tackle is eased off. If it is found to be a problem in light winds then a length of shockcord can be used to pull the car aft.

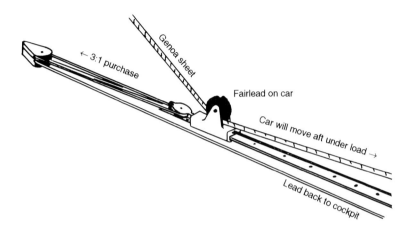

Genoa
REACHING SHEET

One item of portable equipment which I always take when I am preparing to instruct on other people's yachts, is a reaching sheet with snatch block. This device can be used in many different situations; for example to barber-haul the genoa out to the toe-rail or to act as a temporary sheet while changing sails or adjusting the sheet lead.

The reaching sheet itself can be as simple as a length of 12mm braidline, about a boat length long. In this case it would need to be tied to the clew of the sail, not ideal for temporary uses but a hook or snap shackle on the end will greatly enhance its value.

I have used two types of attachment. The open "meat hook" system, of say a Wichard snap shackle with the sprung steel fastener removed has the advantage of being very quick to attach and remove but has the disadvantage of possibly falling off if the sail flaps. The other and probably better type of end fitting is a trigger-latch snap shackle which can be quickly attached or removed but which will not fall off by accident.

The snatch block is a side opening block fixed to a snap shackle which can be attached to the toe rail or to an eye bolt. It allows for quick and easy placement of the reaching sheet and can also be used independently as a temporary sheet lead (eg. For moving the spinnaker lead forward while running) or through which to lead any rope.

Genoa
INBOARD OR OUTBOARD SHEETING ANGLE UPWIND?
It is fairly obvious that the further inboard you have the genoa sheet fairlead, the higher you will be able to point. This is because of the reduced angle between the fully sheeted sail and the boat's centreline. What is not quite so obvious is the effect that the sheeting angle has on the overall sail plan.

When the genoa is sheeted well inboard, it automatically closes the slot between the genoa and the mainsail — good in moderate airs but disastrous when you are either over-canvassed or sailing in very light breezes.

Take the case of the very light breeze first. You must not close the slot too much or you will create a constriction and prevent air getting through the slot, thus stalling the whole rig. Here you may still want to sheet inboard, but with a much looser sheet tension to allow the sail to twist off and open the slot again.

When over-pressed, you need to widen the slot by sheeting further outboard since this allows the mainsail to be dumped further down the traveller track to keep the yacht on her feet. With the genoa sheeted inboard, it is impossible to drop the mainsail down without excessive back winding. Sailing in strong winds is often accompanied by large waves, which mean that you are unable to point as high as in flat water — so once again you can get away with a wider sheeting angle.

In moderate airs, the wind will go through the slot and be accelerated almost without regard to its width, so you might as well have as narrow a sheeting angle as is possible within the constraints of your shroud base and spreader length.

Genoa
TELL-TALES
All headsails, with the possible exception of the storm jib, should have an adequate number of tell-tales to assist trimming. They show when there is airflow over each side of the sail; the windward ones lifting higher and higher and ultimately flapping as the sail is eased (or the helmsman sails at higher angles without the trimmer sheeting in). The leeward tell-tales should

normally stream aft, since once they start to flap or go limp it shows that the sail is stalled.

Since you need tell-tales on both sides of the sail, it is really important to be able to distinguish which is which. There are two easy ways to do this and both methods should be used whenever possible. All tell-tales should be of a dark colour so that you can see them through the thickness of the sailcloth and it is always worth having the ones on the starboard side (say) green and those on the port side (say) red. However in some light conditions it will not be possible to distinguish colours and so the tell-tale on one side should always be higher than that on the other. I like to have all the starboard side tell-tales about two to three centimeters above those on the port side.

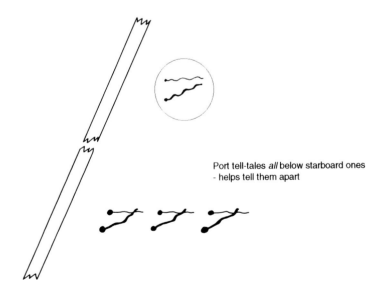

Port tell-tales *all* below starboard ones
- helps tell them apart

Genoa
FORE-AND-AFT SHEET LEAD POSITION

Tell-tales can also be used to indicate when the fore-and-aft sheet lead position is correct. Assuming that you have several sets of tell-tales on the luff of the genoa, in most situations the sail should be trimmed so that they all react at the same time to alterations of wind angle. (But also see page 119.)

Assume that there are just three sets of tell-tales, one about ¼ of the way up the luff, one ½ way up and the top ones about ¾ of the way up. Trim the sail so that the middle set are perfect, with the windward tell-tale straight back and pointing slightly upwards. If the tell-tale on the windward side of the highest set is flapping, then it shows that the top of the sail is under trimmed and the sheet lead needs to go forward. The reverse is true if the tell-tales are stalled.

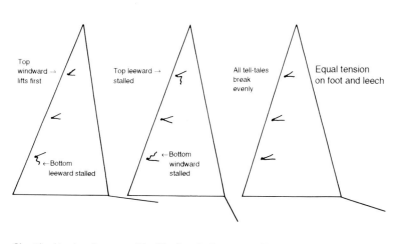

Top windward → lifts first

←Bottom leeward stalled

Sheet lead too far aft

Top leeward → stalled

←Bottom windward stalled

Sheet lead too far forward

All tell-tales break evenly

Equal tension on foot and leech

Sheet lead correct

Genoa
SHEET TENSION

Whatever the sail combination going upwind, there will always be a trade-off between pointing angle and boatspeed. The continual aim should be optimum v.m.g. for the conditions.

So far as the genoa trimmer is concerned this trade-off is represented by sheet tension. As the sheet is eased the helmsman is forced to sail at wider and wider angles but the boatspeed will rise. Conversely if the sheet is wound in tighter, it will enable the yacht to be sailed at a smaller angle to the wind but there will be a corresponding loss in speed.

With small headsails such as the No. 3 or No. 4 the reference for how tight the sheet is, will be its position in relation to the shrouds near the base. Just touching, reasonably firm against the shrouds or really hard. With large overlapping headsails, it is normally the distance of the leech from the spreader ends which is used as a reference. Evenly spaced marks on each spreader end, at 1″ (2.5cm) intervals give a reliable guide as to the distance from the spreader.

In either case, the trimmer must coordinate with the helmsman to ensure that the sail is trimmed for optimum performance. If you have well calibrated instruments that include a v.m.g. readout, it is possible to trim to give the best average v.m.g. over a period of 30 seconds plus.

However you are deciding on the trim, do not forget

about wind shear (see page 122) and wave angle (see page 120), both of which can alter the tack to tack trim.

Mainsail
UPWIND SHEET TENSION

Over the years as a cruising instructor and racing coach, I have frequently gone aboard yachts and watched the mainsheet trimmer. I have then asked him "how do you determine the correct tension to apply when going upwind?". All too often the honest reply is that he doesn't really know. Sometimes it has been little more than the having the vague idea that you need to pull harder when the wind increases.

In actual fact, there is very little mystique about mainsheet tension and if a few basic rules are applied, if you concentrate and don't mind working hard, then you can become a reasonable mainsheet trimmer.

On most racing yachts or cruiser-racers, there will be a mainsheet and a separate mainsheet traveller. In these cases while going upwind, the mainsheet itself is just applying leech tension to the sail.

As we tighten the mainsheet more and more, the amount of twist in the sail will be reduced. This effectively sheets in the top part of the sail harder compared to the bottom. The ideal average tension is that which does not quite stall the sail. (N.B. If the sail is stalled, then less drive is generated and the boat will be slower.) In order to ascertain when this optimum is reached, it is necessary to have tell-tales on the leech of the sail, positioned at the end of each batten pocket. If the sail stalls, then the air flow will break away from the leech and the tell-tale will disappear around the back of the sail. Ideal trim is when the top tell-tale is occasionally breaking, thus showing that the sail is as tight as it can be without being stalled.

We still need different sheet tensions for different wind strengths but this is automatically taken into account by the tell-tales. In light airs, the top tell-tale will break with much less sheet tension than that needed in strong winds and vice-versa.

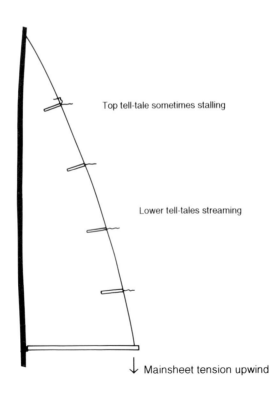

Top tell-tale sometimes stalling

Lower tell-tales streaming

↓ Mainsheet tension upwind

Mainsail
CRACK-OFF FOR SPEED

Mainsheet tension is always a trade-off between speed and pointing. Although having the top tell-tale almost breaking gives a good average setting, there will inevitably be times when you want to point a little higher than normal even if it means that you go slower, while conversely there will be times when you need to foot off a little and increase speed. In the former case, the mainsheet needs to be trimmed a little harder which will partially stall the sail. In the latter case, the sheet can be eased slightly, opening the top of the sail and increasing twist which will allow the boat to foot off faster.

When playing with the mainsail controls in this way never forget that the whole sail plan needs to be trimmed in concert, and you will not achieve the full benefit from adjusting the mainsail unless you trim the genoa at the same time.

Mainsail
TRAVELLER VERSUS
BOOM VANG UPWIND

Many dinghy classes do not have a mainsheet traveller at all but manage to sail upwind very efficiently, whereas nearly all racing yachts have a traveller of some kind. In a dinghy without a traveller, the leech tension is controlled with the boom vang (kicking strap), allowing the mainsheet to act much as a traveller does on a larger boat and letting the whole mainsail in and out like a barn door. Is this a technique which can be applied to yachts as well?

I have used the technique described above, often called "vang sheeting", to great effect on yachts up to about 10 metres but it is a system which calls for considerable skill and great caution. To be effective your boom vang must be very powerful, with a purchase in the order of 32:1 or even greater on most yachts. When sailing upwind in gusty conditions you then have one person playing the vang to adjust the leech tension, with the mainsheet trimmer playing the sheet in the gusts and lulls to avoid excessive weather helm and heel angle. The chief advantage is that you are not restricted to a short traveller or limited by inefficient traveller controls which are found on many cruiser racers.

The system works well BUT:–

1. It puts immense strain on the boom, vang and gooseneck fittings because of the large loads needed to maintain leech tension with a control which is quite near the mast in comparison to the mainsheet.
2. You must ease the vang before bearing away, since to bear away without so doing will probably cause the middle of the mast to be pushed sideways by the boom and may well break the mast.
3. The people playing the boom vang and mainsheet need to work very closely with each other or the sail will not be trimmed effectively.

Mainsail
USE OF BACKSTAY IN GUSTS
Most fractionally rigged yachts can be made to go upwind more effectively in gusty conditions if the top

of the mainsail is flattened in each gust by pulling on the backstay.

If you watch the mainsheet trimmer on a flat out racing yacht such as a One Tonner, you will see that he is not just playing the sheet and traveller controls but is also continually adjusting the backstay. So long as you are able to bend the topmast with your backstay then this should be your aim too.

As a gust hits and the boat starts to heel, the backstay is tightened which flattens and depowers the mainsail at the top while also freeing the leech and allowing the sail to twist off and spill wind. A secondary benefit is that by tightening the backstay, the forestay will also be hardened up a little, thus flattening the front of the genoa and depowering that sail.

If you are unable to play the backstay upwind on your yacht, then it is well worth considering how to change the controls to make this possible.

Spinnaker
AIR FLOW OVER
THE SPINNAKER
When spinnakers were first invented, it was thought that they acted as big wind catching balloons but it was soon realised that this was not the case. The theory now is, that except on a square run, a spinnaker should be treated as an aerofoil. There needs to be air flow from the luff towards the leech and if this is not present then the sail will be stalled and cannot be generating the optimum forward drive.

If you always keep this concept in mind when dealing with the spinnaker, you will find that trimming becomes much easier and more efficient. Any principles which apply to the genoa can also be applied to the spinnaker. The only real difference (apart from cloth weight and area) is that with a genoa, the tack position is fixed and so the sail cannot be properly set once the wind is further aft than about 55°, whereas with a spinnaker, the tack is positioned at the end of the pole. This enables the whole sail to be moved round relative to the wind and therefore the proper airflow can be maintained until on a very broad reach.

Spinnaker
FORE-AND-AFT POLE POSITION

As touched upon in the previous tip, the fore-and-aft position of the spinnaker pole should be continually adjusted to keep the leading edge of the sail pointing into the apparent wind and thus maintaining air flow over both sides of the sail.

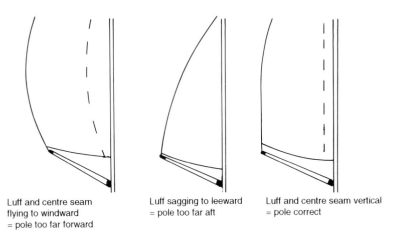

Luff and centre seam
flying to windward
= pole too far forward

Luff sagging to leeward
= pole too far aft

Luff and centre seam vertical
= pole correct

In general terms this will involve setting the pole at right angles to the apparent wind, at least as a starting point. Once the spinnaker is then set and trimmed so that the windward edge is rolling in, the pole can be fine tuned to get the luff rising vertically from the pole end. If the luff sags to leeward from the pole then the pole needs to be eased forward, whereas if the spinnaker luff is trying to fly to windward of the pole end then the pole is not squared back far enough.

Obviously there are limits as to how far the pole can be moved, it cannot be let further forward than the forestay and neither can it be squared back beyond the shrouds. This means that on a very close reach at say 70° to the apparent wind, with the pole just about touching the forestay, the pole will of necessity be over-squared by about 20°. As the wind frees it is important to reduce this over-squaring gradually, so that at say 90° to the apparent wind the pole has been squared back about 10° from the forestay and the pole is not actually square to the apparent wind until the wind is at about 110°.

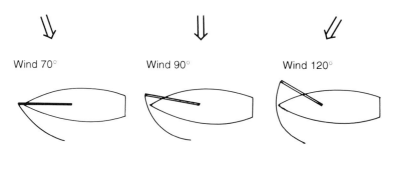

Wind 70°

Wind 90°

Wind 120°

Pole on forestay
= 20° over square

Pole 10° back from forestay
= 10° over square

Pole 30° back from forestay
= square

Spinnaker
POLE HEIGHT

Spinnaker pole height can be adjusted up and down to give the optimum shape. The simplistic approach is to allow the leeward clew to find its own level and then adjust the pole until the two clews are level. This works in a lot of situations but at either end of the wind angle range it leaves a lot to be desired.

A better way to consider pole height is to equate it with halyard tension on a genoa. The lower the pole goes, the tighter the luff will be and thus the draft will move forward as well. As the wind moves forward towards a close reach, so the draft will be dragged aft and thus the pole will need to be lowered in order to maintain maximum draft about 50% of the way from luff to leech.

A good guide for pole height is to trim the spinnaker until it is "on edge" with the luff just curling in and to note where the luff curls first. The ideal will be if it starts to curl at the junction between the vertical panels and the curved shoulders, that is where the panels change from horizontal to vertical on a tri-radial sail. If the point of curl is higher than this, then the pole is too high and vice versa.

Spinnaker
TWEAKERS

The spinnaker sheet lead is normally led right to the aft corner of the yacht, which is great for close reaching situations. On a broad reach or a run, having the lead so far aft will allow the spinnaker leech to twist off excessively and thus lose power in the top sections.

A tweaker system, with a 2:1 purchase set up about amidships will allow for infinite adjustment of the lead position with no problems. Harken make special back-to-back blocks for this purpose for most sizes of yacht, but if you want to utilise existing equipment then any two single blocks can be shackled together.

A less convenient alternative to a tweaker but one which still works, is to have a snatch block which can be clipped to the toe rail and then have the sheet led through it. If this system is employed then it is important to clip the block to the rail and take the sheet down to the fixed block rather than vice versa, or as bitter experience tells me, it is possible to lose control and let the block fly up into your face!

Spinnaker
TRIM FOR A WINDY RUN

When going square downwind on a windy day, getting the ultimate power from your spinnaker may not be the prime requirement. If the spinnaker is trimmed as near to perfection as possible on a run, it will tend to generate a rolling moment which as we all know can increase quickly into death rolls.

There are two reasons for this phenomenon. On a square run it is difficult to maintain constant airflow from luff to leech and it is likely that the airflow will sometimes reverse, thus putting the spinnaker out of balance. The second reason is that with the clews flying fairly high, it is certain that the leeches will twist off when the sail is hit by a gust, causing the head to become unstable.

Slightly over sheeting the sail will get rid of some of the problems and is a good way to temporarily dampen a roll before it gets out of hand, but a better long term method is to strap the spinnaker down somewhat. This is done by lowering the pole and at the same time moving the sheet lead forward, maybe even sheeting with the guy. This tightens both leeches and prevents them from twisting open in the gusts. The downside is that you are not generating so much power, therefore this method should only be used in situations when handling the yacht has become a problem.

Spinnaker
CONCENTRATION

Almost anyone can become a good spinnaker trimmer once they have gained an understanding of the basic principles involved, but some trimmers are consistently faster than others. Having watched countless trimmers at work, I am convinced that the difference is simply the degree of concentration that is put into the job.

We all know that "Sod's Law" will ensure that the spinnaker collapses every time the trimmer looks around to admire the view but this is only the tip of an iceberg. The trimmer needs to be considering sheet tension, pole position fore-and-aft, pole height and wind angle all the time and he needs to be relating all these factors to the boatspeed. To do this properly the trimmer needs to be in a position where he can see the whole of the sail and he needs to concentrate all the time.

He needs to have a good working partnership with the helmsman so that they are continually aiming at the same targets speeds or wind angles and so that they both know and understand the problems being experienced by each other. For example, tacking downwind in light airs there will be a constant desire by the helmsman to aim further downwind and he must be encouraged to do so whenever there is good pressure in the sail but he must be told to come up again as soon as the pressure decreases — before the speed drops too much.

General
DRAFT POSITION

In basic terms, all sails work by acting as an aerofoil, with the curve of the sails creating differential pressures over the windward and leeward sides. The sail maker will have designed the sail to have a particular optimum shape but because the sails are made from cloth which can be stretched, this shape takes considerable work to maintain. With the air flow over the sail normally being from the luff towards the leech, the sail will be stretched backwards by the pressure of the wind whenever it increases or the apparent wind angle goes forward. Although modern sail materials and construction methods reduce this effect, it is still visible even on a Kevlar/Mylar sail.

The method used to return the shape of the sail to its proper position is luff tension. Halyard tension with the genoa, a combination of halyard and cunningham with the mainsail and pole height with the spinnaker. As the luff is stretched tighter, this draws material from the back of the sail further forwards and thus moves the draft forward.

Maximum draft 45% back from genoa luff - correct luff tension

NB - Mainsail should have maximum draft at 50-55%

Halyard too slack - draft aft

Halyard too tight - draft too far forward

As a general rule, the maximum draft in a genoa needs to be just forward of the middle when going upwind and about in the middle when reaching, while that of the mainsail needs to be in the middle when going upwind and maybe slightly aft of the middle when off the wind. The draft in a spinnaker will need to be about in the middle in most circumstances.

The draft position is usually expressed in terms of the percentage from luff towards the leech, so a sail with the draft in the middle will be said to have its draft "50% of the way back", while a genoa with the maximum draft just forward of the middle may have its draft "45% of the way back".

General
DRAFT POSITION — SPECIAL CASES
Although it is usually best to position the point of maximum draft roughly in the middle of the sail, there will be times when you may need either a more rounded or a flatter entry than normal.

If sailing in relatively large waves for the wind strength or in very shifty wind, it will be difficult to stay at a constant angle to the wind and therefore it will be hard to keep the tell-tales on the genoa streaming. The flatter the entry, the harder this problem will become since with a very flat entry the sail will either be set right or wrong with no half measures. A sail which is set with a tighter luff and therefore a more rounded entry will be much more forgiving. You will be able to keep the tell-tales more or less working even with the apparent wind angle changing by a few degrees. This principle is just as true for spinnaker trimming as it is for the genoa.

It has to be remembered that having a rounded entry does mean that your pointing ability will suffer somewhat, therefore be careful not to overdo luff tension. In flat water and steady wind, it is possible to sail with the halyard really slack, giving a flat entry and thus allowing the yacht to point significantly higher.

Tight halyard to give a rounder entry in steep or choppy seas

Slack halyard to give a flat entry for high pointing in smooth water

General
TWIST IN WAVES

While sailing in flat water the trimmers will be striving to keep the sails lifting evenly throughout their height, adjusting the genoa sheet lead or the mainsheet tension to keep the tell-tales streaming together. When sailing upwind in waves this is no longer possible. If you have the sail trimmed as it would be for flat water, no part of it will ever actually be trimmed correctly.

As the bow rises up a wave, the movement of the boat

will generate a wind from astern which will serve to bring the apparent wind aft and decrease it. Conversely, when pitching forward down the wave, this will generate a forward component into the apparent wind which will be brought forward and increased. As well as allowing for this by steering into the wind when going up the wave and away from the wind when pitching forward, the trim of the sails needs to be adjusted to take into account the changing apparent wind angles and strengths.

Moving the genoa sheet lead aft a notch or so and at the same time allowing the main boom to rise slightly will let both sails twist off to leeward at the top more than usual. This will mean that the bottom part of the sail will work efficiently when pitching forward, with a narrower angle to the apparent wind, while the top of the sails will be under sheeted and will spill wind. This combination will keep you driving forward without increasing the heeling force too much. Then as the bow rises up the next wave and the apparent wind decreases and moves aft, the top of the sails will start working better, giving power high up but since the wind will be weaker, this once again should not make the boat heel excessively.

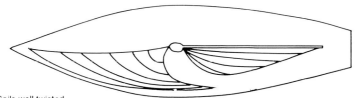

Sails well twisted
(genoa car back and main sheet eased)
Allows the top of the sail to work when the boat pitches up
and the bottom to work when pitching down in waves.

General
WIND SHEAR

Even for those who do not know much about meteorology, it is fairly obvious that the wind near the surface will be affected more by drag than wind higher up, away from the land or waves. This means that unless there is mixing of the higher and lower air masses, such as on a day with good convection and cumulus clouds, the air near the surface will travel more slowly than air higher up. The result is that the wind at the masthead will often be stronger than the wind near the bottom of the sails.

A less obvious fact is that the spin of the earth imparts just enough turning force into the wind so that where the air has been affected more by the drag of the earth's surface, it will be changed in direction as well as in strength. In the northern hemisphere, this means that on a day with little mixing of low and high air, the air higher up will be veered (turned to the right) compared with the wind low down.

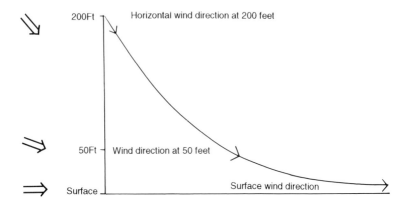

The effect that this has on sailing is very important. Assuming that we are sailing in the northern hemisphere, it means that on a day when there is wind shear, the wind at the top of the sails on starboard tack will be much freer than the wind low down and vice versa on port tack. This means that the sails will need much more twist on starboard tack to keep the tell-tales flying evenly, than on port tack and indeed, the speed differences tack to tack can be quite amazing.

General
LEECH LINES

Most racing sails have a leech line. This is located inside the leech tabling and can be tightened to remove leech flutter whenever necessary. It is important to realize that when you tighten the leech line you are in effect making up for small imperfections in the shape of the sail and the differential stretch of the sail in varying wind strengths. The leech line should only be tightened JUST ENOUGH to stop the sail fluttering and should be eased whenever possible. If it is left permanently taut, then the back end of the sail will be hooked to windward and will be slow. If your sail needs so much leech line applied that it looks hooked, then it is time to send it back to the sail maker to have the joining seams on the leech adjusted to remove unwanted stretch.

Make sure that you can adjust the leech lines on your sails easily and that they do not get caught up when tacking. Plastic jamming cleats are never strong enough and should be replaced by metal cleats on heavy sails, while Velcro works well on the light genoa. On larger yachts, it is worth considering having the mainsail leech line taken round a block at the head of the sail and then back down the luff to the tack, since this allows simple adjustment on all points of sail.

Index

Admiral's Cup   18, 35
apparent wind   31, 51,
    60, 120

back bearing   50
backstay   111
barging   14
bear-away set   34
bearing   50
beat   15, 33, 38
bias   48, 56
boatspeed   59
boom vang   109

calibration   59
chart case   45
chart table   40
charts   40, 43
clear air   24
clearing line   51
clutch   69
collision   32
colour coding   66
compass   57
compression load
    99
cover   21, 33
cross-tide   50

death rolls   115
Decca   61

dirty air   33
draft   118
    position   119

echo sounder   57
entry   119

fairlead   100,102
finishing line   56
foredeck   73

genoa   57, 73, 78, 100,
    105, 112, 121
genoa sheet   72
GPS   61
gust   33, 111
guy   72, 77
gybe   36, 71, 77, 78, 93
    mark 34
gybe-set   34, 82
gybing angles   56

halyard   66, 73, 79
hand-bearing compass
    49
hull speed   29

instruments   57

kicking strap   109

lay-line   17, 19
lee bow tack   22
leech line   123
leeward mark   34, 37
Loran C   61
light airs   85
luff, to   25,38
luff tension   73, 118

mainsail   57, 99, 103,
  107
mainsheet   109
making tack   21
mark rounding   38
mast   88, 94, 97
  -rake 95
mast-abeam   25

navigation   40

offshore   41
overlap   18, 35, 36
overtake   25, 35

plotting board   40
polar curves   55
position line   50
prebend   98
proper course   15, 27
protest   18, 32, 35

racing rules   14
rating   55

reach   24, 32, 86, 113
reaching sheet   101
rhumb line   51
riding turn   80
run   33, 89, 115

sailing instructions   41
sea breeze   48
sheet   72, 77
  tension   107
  angle   102
shroud   97
  tension   97
side deck   40
slot   103
snatch block   102, 115
snap shackle   75
spinnaker   34, 64, 73, 76,
  78, 86, 114
spinnaker hoist   71
  pole   70, 114
  stops   65
spreaders   99
square wind
direction   49
start   12, 14, 48, 50
starting line   12,49
stern wave   29
surf   31

tell-tales   57, 92, 103,
  108, 119
tidal wind   53

126

tide   52
tide   52
topping lift   70, 78
tow   27, 29
transit   50
traveller   88, 103, 109
trip line   70
true wind   54
turtle   64
tweakers   114
twist   120

velocity made good   58
  prediction 55

waypoint   61
weather helm   95, 110
wind direction   47
  bend   48
  shadow   25
  shear   60, 122
windshift   33, 47
windward mark   17, 34, 45, 48

Other books in the *Tips from the Top* series

Chisnell on Instrument Techniques by Mark Chisnell
How to put all the instruments on a modern boat to
their best use.
Publication January '92.
ISBN 1 85310 311 X

Cunliffe on Cruising by Tom Cunliffe
Really practical tips to help the cruising yachtsman.
ISBN 1 85310 301 2

Also from *Waterline*

Boatwords by Denny Desoutter
Over 1500 boating terms explained in the author's
entertaining style.
ISBN 1 85310 299 7

Hand, Reef and Steer by Tom Cunliffe
Traditional seamanship for classic boats.
Publication January '92.
ISBN 1 85310 309 8

Going About Cruising by Andrew Simpson
An introduction to cruising for consenting adults.
Publication January '92.
ISBN 1 85310 293 8

Write for a complete catalogue of Waterline Books to
101 Longden Road, Shrewsbury SY3 9EB, England.